THE BEING ENTREPRENEUR

An inside out approach to entrepreneurship

Mark Vandeneijnde

Copyright © 2020 Mark Vandeneijnde
All rights reserved.
ISBN: 9798679381537

DEDICATION

To the change agents, the dreamers, and the inspired leaders
Who choose to courageously build the bridge
To a world their heart knows is possible

Contents

Acknowledgments i
Introduction 1
1. My journey into business 4
2. Glimpse beyond the veil 11
3. A new world is visible, but I'm not in it yet 21
4. I'm in it and that's all I can see 29
5. Departure 37
6. Transformation & apprenticeship 47
7. All the dots connect 70
8. Building the bridge 78
9. Back to source 101

Acknowledgments

Thank you to my wife, Feiyin Situ, for your patience and the freedom you have given me to pursue this dream

Thank you to my kids, Oscar and Audrey, for your unconditional belief in me and intuitive understanding of what I've been up to all these years

Thank you to my friend and co-creator, Sujith Ravindran, for the manifestation power you brought to our visions

Thank you to the immensely talented community of coaches who continue to inspire me on this co-creative adventure

Introduction

When the old comes to an end and the new is not yet fully within reach, we find ourselves in a space in between. It's an uncomfortable, but also a rich creative place to be. I once again find myself "in between" and am taking the opportunity to step back, reflect and share some lessons learned from the past 10 years of Being Entrepreneurship.

The idea to write this book has been there for many years now. Quite early on, I knew this entrepreneurial journey that I was on, was different than most. It was fueled from a place of inner conviction. My inner voice was nudging me in a certain direction but there wasn't an explicit need in the marketplace for what I had to offer. This of course goes against typical best practices when it comes to launching a new venture.

Traditionally, entrepreneurs start with identifying an opportunity in the market and then apply their unique skill sets or experiences to create innovative solutions that appeal to their target group. Many books have been written to support this kind of entrepreneurship and I'm sure this approach will continue to fuel great progress in the future.

However, there are not many resources or best practices for people like me who choose to walk the inner path of entrepreneurship. I learned early on that applying typical business building principles would not work for the adventure I had committed to. I also realized that the lessons I was learning (sometimes the hard way) were not just unique to my experience, they seemed to also resonate with other like-minded entrepreneurs. This is when I decided that one day, when all the dots had connected, I would write this book and tell the story of the Being Entrepreneur.

June 6th, 2019

My heart beats with anticipation as I finally sit down to write the first lines of this story. I can feel the intensity of each individual experience over the past 10+ years culminate into this point in time. I can now see how every single step, even the painful ones, have led to a very unique entrepreneurial journey that I now know needs to be shared.

In the years leading up to 2010 I could feel a deep calling coming through me. At first it was a whisper that could easily be ignored but with time that voice became clearer and bolder to the point where I was catapulted into action. The adventure of a lifetime had begun. It has taken me to unimaginable places where I have felt stretched way beyond my comfort zone yet chose to say "yes" to many seemingly impossible projects and ideas. Of all the unimaginable places I had to explore and discover, the one that stands out most is the place deep inside myself - the Inner Being.

So much of what I had experienced as "real" until then had to be reexamined and eventually deconstructed to a profound core. Many of the stories that had shaped my life until then could now be left behind. I was free to change "the rules of the game" and, in doing so, I started to craft a new story. This is the story of the Being Entrepreneur.

1. My journey into business

The journey of a Being Entrepreneur starts long before we graduate from college or walk away from a 9-5 job with our 'big idea'. It starts when we first become aware of the deeper meaning of our unique life experiences, and recognize how the different 'dots of our lives' connect to inform our entrepreneurial adventures.

Many years ago, when I was 15 or 16, my father told me a story that shaped the rest of his life. He was my age at the time and had a passion and talent for art. His dream was to go to art school so that one day he could make a living doing what he loves doing. His father, of course having the best interest of his son in mind, but also projecting some of his own fears, made the argument that his love for art should be kept a hobby. Instead, the more responsible choice that he was encouraged to make was to go to business school.

I grew up seeing my father fully at peace with the choices he had made. He became a very well-respected international businessman, provided comfortably for his family and continued to nurture his passion for art by taking evening classes. His commitment and dedication to keeping this hobby alive was an inspiration to me. At sixteen I could see the wisdom in my grandfather's words. And so, after graduating from high school, I simply assumed that business school was the right choice for me too.

I don't remember having many doubts about that. Nor do I remember a deeper passion drawing me into another direction. Although it appeared to me that I was doing the responsible thing by following my father's footsteps, there was of course one important difference. I did not have a passionate hobby to give a sense of meaning to my day-to-day life. I was trying to follow a recipe, but I didn't have all the right ingredients. The spices were missing.

Not only did I lack the drive and ambition to be successful in that world, I also was not a particularly good student. My grades were average, yet when the moment came to pass my final mathematics exam of the International Baccalaureate Program, I got the second highest grade in the school. It was as if I had had a brief moment of enlightenment where everything clicked, and I was able to access abilities reserved only to the top tier students.

This magical performance was sufficient to get me into one of the top business schools in North America. However, this achievement did not do much to boost my confidence or desire to be in business. Instead I continued to deliver good enough results with the hope this would land me a respected job and make my family (my Dad in particular) proud. After graduation, a nice but not particularly prestigious job with a small computer company, landed in my lap.

While I was an account manager for a small Value-Added Reseller in the computer business, I saw my business school colleagues join the ranks of large consulting firms, travelling the world and making "good" money. They were living the business student dream, taking life in their own hands. Meanwhile I felt like I was playing small, simply going with the flow and letting life take me wherever it wanted. I was no longer on the fast track to success.

My boss at the time tried to convince me that being a big fish in a small pond was better than a small fish in a big pond but that didn't satisfy me. I wanted bigger and better. My idea of success was now firmly rooted in the stories of the people around me rather than based on my own personal standards and aspirations. That inner work was not something I was ready for then. It was much easier to look for the solution elsewhere. So, I decided to go back to school to get my MBA. Surely with a master's degree in hand I would be able to find the success I was looking for.

Again, all the right doors opened effortlessly. I (barely) passed the GMAT test but it was sufficient to get me into the one-year MBA program in Leuven, Belgium. By the end of the year I had a job offer with one of the largest and most respected consumer goods companies in the world. It wasn't outstanding grades that made this possible, nor was it my wealth of experience. Instead, it boiled down to an essay I wrote as part of the application process for a student internship program.

I remember taking this assignment quite lightly. In my mind there was no real chance that such a company, reputed for recruiting the best talent, would consider me. So I decided to write the essay from a place of having nothing to lose. I don't recall the exact topic, but I do remember being authentic in what I wrote. It must have been another brief moment of brilliance that I unconsciously tapped into because what came through was real, vulnerable and brimming with ideas and possibilities. When dropping it at the post office I knew it would be polarizing. Either they love it, or it will land in the crazy bucket. It was perhaps one of the first times that I deliberately showed more of my real self and trusted that taking this risk would lead to something good. I also remember it being fun to take this playful and unconventional approach.

Sure enough, a couple of weeks later, I received a letter back from. They decided I was not the right fit for the internship. Not because I was under qualified but because I was OVER qualified! They apparently loved my essay so much that they wanted me to come in directly to interview for a permanent job. I was shocked and could not believe my luck. At some level I felt like a fraud, not trusting that I would be able to consistently deliver the brilliance they had seen in me.

Indeed, after my first year in the company, I was struggling to find my place as an Interactive Marketing Manager for the Benelux region. During my first performance review, the director who had hired me, clearly stated his disappointment. The creative visionary he had met during the interview wasn't showing up for work. And he was right, to a large extent I was overwhelmed by the technical nature of the job as I had no IT and systems background.

I was also in awe of all the fast talking, fast thinking managers around me. From my perspective it seemed like they had everything figured out. I was not up to par - at least that was the story I was telling myself. This left me feeling isolated and incompetent. The performance review therefore came as a wakeup call. I better break out of the funk fast or else my days there would be over soon.

So, I stepped out of my cocoon and started doing what I do best - thinking out of the box. So much of what I saw could be improved. It was as if the pendulum had swung completely the other way. I was envisioning all sorts of new ways we could use digital technologies to build relationships between the large portfolio of well-respected brands and their consumers. I was having lots of fun in this creative space, but it didn't do much to improve my standing within the company. To most people I had stepped way beyond my area of responsibility and expertise. Brand building and concept development was "owned" by the marketing function so who was I as a young IT manager to come and offer my ideas. It didn't matter if they were good or bad, I simply didn't have the credibility to play in that league.

One conversation in particular will always stay with me. My boss at the time, trying to put me back in my well defined area of responsibility, sat me down one day to offer the following piece of advice: "Whatever idea you can think of, no matter how great you think it is, believe me, we already thought about it or it's already been done". That was a huge blow and still today brings me to tears when I think about it. It was becoming clear to my bosses that I was an inadequate fit for the IT function and most probably also for the company.

What followed was a couple of months of nothing. There were no projects for me to work on but there was also no compelling reason to fire me. This place in between was very strange as I remember staying home or coming into work only for a few hours per day, and still getting paid. Nobody was missing me, and nothing was expected of me. In hindsight I realize that it may have been a deliberate tactic to help me move on. The more frustrated and isolated I felt, the more likely I would decide to leave on my own. Sure enough, I was slowly getting to the point where writing this short stint off felt like the only option. My belief of being a fraud was reinforced by the day.

Then, one day, out of the blue I got a call from an IT boss who I hadn't worked with directly but apparently had been observing me from a distance. He had seen something in me that others didn't and rather than try to reshape the IT job to make me fit a bit better, he had the idea of moving me to another function within the company where my skills would be more valued. It was such a simple idea, but it took a deep level of care and courage by that person to put me, as a human being, at the center of the job matching process.

What unfolded from there is a fulfilling 10-year career in the CMK (Consumer and Market Knowledge) function. In hindsight I can see how this one person helped open a door that led me down an incredibly adventurous path, eventually bringing me to where I am today. I hope one day I can find this person again and share the profound impact that his compassion and care had on the rest of my life.

QUESTIONS FOR THE BEING ENTREPRENEUR:

- What were you like as a child? What were your hopes and dreams?

- Do you recognize any beliefs, habits or patterns that were passed on to you by your parents? What impact did they have on your choices while growing up?

- As you become more aware of how your past has shaped the present, what new insights are revealed?

2. Glimpse beyond the veil

A Being Entrepreneur pays close attention to the moments when life is in flow. At first these peak experiences may seem random but when looking deeper we realize they are simply a result of fully living into our true self.

On my journey of self-realization, I have learnt that we can only see what we are ready to see at any given point in time. These "glimpses" serve as clues to show us the next step on our path. It's easy to write them off as random "peak experiences", and nothing more. However, I am discovering that they are all key pieces of a much larger puzzle.

One of the responsibilities we have as Being Entrepreneurs is to assemble these different pieces so that eventually we can start seeing the bigger picture of our life. The moment it "clicks" is the moment we connect the dots of seemingly random peak experiences into a more holistic plan. It's also the moment our life is infused with a deep sense of meaning and purpose. From this place we can access all the energy and inspiration we need to realize our greatest potential. Are you ready to step on the path of a Being Entrepreneur and realize your full creative potential?

In this chapter I will share some of the more significant "glimpses" that I experienced along the way. Some of them happened during my time in business and others long before.

Back in the early 90's, after a long day at university, my roommate and childhood friend would pick me up and drive us to the fringes of the city. Our "spot" was always a quiet, secluded place with a view so we could watch the city come to rest from a distance. As it slowed down, so did we and inevitably amazing conversations would unfold. For years we would do this, often many nights per week. In these moments we consistently experienced a profound immersion into our true selves.

At the time we did not talk about it in this way, we could simply feel the grace of these moments where we shared openly and vulnerably about all aspects of our life. We experienced deep listening and connection with nature, sometimes sitting for long periods of time in complete silence. Inevitably profound new insights would emerge that helped us see new ways forward whenever we felt stuck. We would often come to clear conclusions, make choices, and commit to actions that took our lives into significantly new directions. Even though our friends and family did not really know what we were up to, they often benefited from the new clarity and heightened awareness that we brought back into our day-to-day lives. We were showing up with greater perspective and therefore could engage others in more thoughtful and compassionate ways.

These late-night escapades carried on throughout the 90's, long before I had ever heard of the concept of coaching - long before I could even imagine creating a business and making a living from this. It seems so clear now but back then I could only see what I was ready to see. I could only know what I was ready to know.

The next story takes place around the same time. I was in the middle of my bachelor's degree in Commerce and living in Vancouver. One day a university classmate invited me to join him for a creative writing class. After an initial pushback, I eventually showed up for the first class curious, but doubtful, if I would be able to produce anything of value.

The very first exercise was to write about a childhood memory and be as descriptive as possible within a 10-minute limit. Having this time constraint was a great way to switch off the mind and the critical voice. It forced us to write without censoring or over-thinking. We then spent the rest of the class reading out what we wrote and listening to each other's stories. There was no critical feedback or advice offered. Simply a deep acknowledgment of the unique experiences we each brought to the class. This went way beyond what I expected the class to be. It was as much, or more, about our personal growth as it was about perfecting our writing skills. I felt completely at home in this space and was already looking forward to the next assignment. A few classes later, I was fully in the grove. When asked to write a short story, what emerged would have implications way beyond the class.

I started writing about a young man (more or less my age) who was preparing the last bits and pieces before flying to Tucson Arizona to visit an old girlfriend from high school. They hadn't seen or heard from each other for many years. However, there were still loose ends that hadn't been addressed before going their separate ways. Seeking closure, but not knowing at all what would happen when he arrived, this young man decided to step into the unknown.

Of course, the young man represented me, the only difference was that I had no intention to embark on this adventure to Arizona, at least not when I started writing. As the story unfolded, I started to embody the adventurous spirit of the young man I was describing. Slowly it became clear this was a trip I had to make and discover for myself what would unfold rather than imagining it through a character.

There ended up being three parts to this story. The first one was fictional where I simply imagined what somebody would feel before going on such a trip. The second part was a real account of what happened during my days in Arizona and the third one was a reflection on all the lessons learned once I was back home.

In writing up this story and sharing it with my friends, I was surprised by the extent to which it inspired them. My boss at the time recognized a lot of himself in the story. He was so moved by the adventure and all the lessons learned that he decided to pay for my flight to Arizona and not count my days away as holidays.

I was starting to see the impact my writing and actions could have on others. It felt great but there was an element of randomness to it. In these peak moments I was unaware that I was in fact expressing my true authentic self and living into my full potential. These constructs were unknown to me at the time therefore it was easy to write them off as one-time events - a stroke of genius if you like. I did not have a framework yet to understand what was happening and why I was feeling such fulfillment in those moments. Without this it is very difficult to replicate and sustainably create a life with such intensity and meaning.

In the subsequent chapters these building blocks will become clear but before that, one more story that has proven to be a critical step along the way.

This takes place in 2005 about halfway into my consumer researcher career. I was working on the European Laundry business which meant I would spend a considerable amount of time immersed in the day-to-day lives of consumers to deeply understand how they felt about the laundry product and all the different (little) ways in which it was improving their life. I would then work closely with the brand manager to translate these insights into new product or communication ideas.

What was unique about this brand manager compared to the others I had worked with is that he didn't see me as just the "insights guy". On the surface it might not seem significantly different but in fact it made all the difference. As a function, marketing (i.e. brand managers) were in charge of crafting new ideas and driving them forward in the organization. Insights people like myself were an important contributor to that process but at the end of the day we were not expected (and often not encouraged) to make the leap from insight to idea. There was a clear hierarchy in the system that should be respected.

What was different about this brand manager is not that he couldn't come up with good ideas himself, he simply understood that good ideas could come from anywhere in the organization. So rather than limit people to their functional expertise, he saw us in our wholeness.

Recognizing that I was the kind of person who loved to ideate, he actively encouraged and invited me into strategic brand building meetings (normally off limits for somebody in my role).

What was also special about this person is that he would always make sure that my contributions would be visible to the higher levels of management. He would proactively showcase my unique value add. This was quite uncommon in a highly competitive work environment but in fact it made a lot of sense. Not only did I feel valued and inspired to stretch my contribution even further, but the brand manager became known as one of the best leaders and team builders in the company. He embodied an abundant mindset and deeply believed that by helping me shine, he would inevitably shine as well. To this day it is still one of the most fulfilling work experiences I have ever had. I knew something magical was happening but again couldn't yet explain why and didn't know how to replicate it in a sustainable way.

The following is an example of peak creativity shining through when I would spontaneously step beyond the narrow confines of my job description and think expansively about the opportunities for the business.

Laundry insights from Ryanair flight 88

This summer I took my first Ryanair flight. It was from Brussels to Carcassonne. Actually, to be more precise, it was from Brussels South (otherwise known as Charleroi) to Carcassonne. The 29.99 euros I paid seemed like a great deal but after the hour drive to Charleroi, then the 15 min shuttle bus from the parking lot to the airport, then the long lines at the check-in counter and then finally the uncomfortable wait in a small room just off the tarmac, I wondered if this was not all a big mistake.

As we took off, I forgot about the little hassles, settled in and started to ask myself what made this experience so unique and why everyone around me was so excited. I couldn't help but feel this incredible buzz in the airplane, the kind that only happens when the people, and the environment they are in, are completely in sync. So, although I did not connect with the environment, Ryanair had created the perfect atmosphere and experience for their target consumer. I was intrigued and decided to dedicate the next one and a half hours to uncover this magic formula. The trip had turned into a mini research project, one that I hope will provide deeper insights into the low tier laundry consumers and offer ideas on how we can better appeal to them with our laundry brands in the future.

Here are the 5 key insights that I believe are just as relevant for our Brands as they are for Ryanair

1. **No fuss about comfort, safety and food, just get me there**: Everything about the Ryanair experience is basic. It's almost as simple as taking a bus: you buy a ticket, wait for a while and then push your way in so you can find yourself a good seat. Although it is basic, it is not just about low cost. It's also about getting you there in time and making sure your luggage doesn't get lost. Sounds pretty straightforward but their overall performance on these attributes is best in class and they take every opportunity to tell people about it (for example on the overhead bin doors).
2. **Entertain me:** They play young, energetic music to get the adrenaline flowing before take-off. Then once in the air, a happy steward announces that they will be coming by to sell you everything you could ever dream of: from food and duty free to packaged tours and tombola tickets. The amazing thing is that for once you see people actually buying all this "useless stuff". I am not sure if it is the good mood that they are in, or the feeling that they have saved so much on the ticket price

that is triggering this impulse behavior. Whatever it is, Ryanair is making up for the low-ticket prices. After all the sales commotion, there's a little quiet time to sit back and browse through the Ryanair magazine which features entertaining articles about the cities they fly to as well as fun, quirky facts that you just need to know (like the number of nudist tourists that visited Croatia in 2004).

3. **Give me peace of mind once I arrive in this foreign place**: Not knowing where to stay and what exactly to do when arriving in these foreign cities, where the people speak a different language, is a big barrier to travel for the Ryanair customer. Therefore, Ryanair does everything to make the planning of the trip as easy as possible. On their website you can book cars, hotels and tours. You can buy insurance, travel guides and money. And if you are really new to travelling you can even find out why one would want to travel in the first place under "the reasons to travel section". Not surprisingly, football is one of the key ones.

4. **Make me feel like I am getting a good deal**: Ryanair doesn't actually want to get you from A to B in the cheapest possible way. They just want to create the impression that you are getting the best deal. I am convinced that once you factor in all the little extras purchased on the plane as well the parking fees (it cost me more to park my car in some field 10km away from the airport than to fly back and forth to Carcassonne) you end up paying almost as much as you would with Lufthansa.

5. **Talk to me in a way that I understand**: To sum it all up, Ryanair deeply understands their target traveler. Everything they do is meticulously designed to create the right atmosphere and experience. Everything they communicate is said in a way that connects and makes their traveler feel understood.

Implications for our low-tier laundry Brands:

1. **Superior basic benefits**: Are there any basic category benefits (similar to most punctual) that we can claim superiority on? For example: clothes look new longest (due to lower cleaning performance / cheaper formula)
2. **Entertain**: What more can we do to entertain beyond crazy scent experiences? How about a promotion where we offer Ryanair miles for every purchase? This could be a great way to drive both trial and loyalty. Or what about a print campaign that gives tips on how to have more fun while doing the laundry, or quirky facts about laundry?
3. **Peace of mind**: We need to make the laundry as hassle free as possible. Can we create a product that would allow mixing of colors and whites in a risk-free way? Or one that helps clothes dry faster?
4. **Improve the value perception without being the cheapest**: What font types communicate value? Do bright obnoxious colors mean something must be cheap? How about communicating everyday low price on our packs?
5. **Talk their language when and where they are most receptive**: How can we be more light-hearted and fun? Can we use even simpler and clearer language / demos in our concepts and advertising? Can we use other media (as Ryanair does with the overhead bins) to reach our target in a cheaper and more effective way?

QUESTIONS FOR THE BEING ENTREPRENEUR:

- What are some examples of "peak experiences" in your life?

- Who were you being in those moments? Which inner qualities were fully alive?

- What kind of impact did these peak experiences have on the people around you?

3. A new world is visible, but I'm not in it yet

A Being Entrepreneur embraces all aspects of the self, even the ones that we may wish to avoid or overcome. In my case it was my sensitivity. For most of my life I experienced it as a nuisance until one day it became the greatest gift.

I have a vague memory of a period in my life, I was probably 11 or 12 years old, when I would pray every night before going to sleep. In my prayers I would vividly bring to mind all the people who I could imagine suffering in the world. Some of these images came from the evening news reporting on wars around the world and others might have come from friends or family members who I knew were struggling at home. I easily picked up on other people's pain and my way of processing it at the time was to hold all of it in my awareness and simply ask the "higher powers" for help.

Many years later, somewhere around 2007, I was introduced to the concept of HSP, which stands for Highly Sensitive Person. I didn't know at the time, but these three letters would eventually bring tremendous chaos as well as tremendous meaning into my life. The friend who had seen some HSP characteristics in me gifted me the following book: The Power of Sensitivity, by Ted Zeff.

I remember having a profound feeling of coming home when reading it. It didn't take long before I was fully absorbed in this highly unusual way of describing a certain segment of society. The author understood the deepest layers of my Being. He was able to put into words and make sense of the rich, but often confusing, inner world that was at the source of how I was experiencing life. My soul was starting to be exposed and as a result I now had more awareness on what had given spark to the magical moments described in chapter two.

What I had previously thought of as moments of enlightenment or peak experiences, were now a natural consequence of my inner being shining its light. This was a profound awakening. It helped me realize that as human beings we often have more power than we think we do to create wonder-filled lives.

Even though this awareness was helping me to connect dots that previously seemed random, my day-to-day reality was still lagging behind. Whenever I was around a lot of people, I would quickly feel overwhelmed. My senses could not handle the sheer quantity of stimulus coming my way as part of working in an open space office environment. My attention was constantly being drawn away by the busyness of all the people around me. It seemed like I was the only one not thriving in this fast-paced, doing-focused workplace. My natural response was to hide in the nearby meeting or huddle rooms. This helped me focus but after a while I also felt isolated and disconnected from my colleagues.

During performance review time, the feedback would invariable be about not speaking up enough and needing to be more effective at engaging others. It boiled down to "leadership". No matter how hard I tried, the impulse to speak up and stand out from the crowd would never last long. It wasn't me and therefore reinforced my sense of inadequateness. Rather than open up and motivate me, it actually closed me down even further. I remember times when I simply wanted to be invisible and disappear. I had found one or two toilets, removed from the busy zones of the office, where I could sit in stillness and darkness. In these moments I would find some momentary peace.

Another coping mechanism was to "sneak" out of the building and go on an extended walk, sometimes for several hours in a row. I think I had gotten quite good at being invisible because I would rarely get questions from my colleagues about where I was. I guess that's the advantage of working in a big company. I was a small fish swimming in a big pond so as long as my work got done, there seemed to be a lot I could get away with. Of course, feeling inadequate, and often quite useless at the end of the day, was a high price to pay for this seemingly relaxed work arrangement.

Finding out about HSP made me feel better. It helped me understand that there wasn't anything "wrong" with me. Acknowledging that I was OK was a first important step. I wasn't quite ready to see it as a gift yet but at least now I wouldn't beat myself up for retreating into the dark toilets or going on an extended lunch walk around the office. I could see these as important self-care activities so I could better handle the busyness of the workplace. I also stopped driving into work and instead made walking a part of my daily practice. The 45-minute walk was the perfect way to get inspired in the morning and then unwind in the evening. Incorporating these habits into my life is what allowed me to survive, and at times thrive, in this corporate environment.

This was also the time when I first discovered coaching. Of course, I was familiar with the idea of a sports coach, but a life coach was a totally new concept to me. I loved that it was different from mentoring or counselling. It immediately made sense to me that answers to all our deepest questions lie within us rather than with somebody else, no matter how wise or experienced the other person is. Like HSP, this was another piece of the puzzle. It validated something I had felt deep inside but the world around me mostly told a very different story. At school, 90% of the learning is sourced from textbooks and dependent on a well-defined curriculum. Very seldom are we encouraged to trust our own inner knowing to navigate and make sense of the world. Coaching might not be the optimal way of learning maths or history, but it certainly is the way to go if we want more clarity on our own values, principles and purpose in life.

But how do we transcend all the noise and past conditioning on who we SHOULD be to reach that pure level of inner truth, a place of unequivocal clarity about who we are and why we are here? And how do we then resculpt our life around this deep inner knowing?

In my case it meant finding a coach who could support me in this process. My search across the world wide web led me to an HSP coach based in California. Right from the start of our six-month program, the coach took me on a visualization into the future. In this deep meditative state, I was introduced to my future self - the person I had become five years in the future. It wasn't just a linear projection of who I was today, instead it was a version of myself that had grown exponentially into his greatest potential. I literally had the opportunity to sit down with my future self for tea and ask him anything I wanted.

In this process I got a deeper glimpse into who I had become, the environment I was in, the people I was around and the overall energy of the moment. I remember feeling welcomed by a very peaceful and calm person, somebody who exuded a great confidence and had found a way to integrate his deeper self in all aspects of his life. Although all the impressions were very subtle in nature, I knew it was in the realm of possibility. Nothing felt more true and real at that moment in time. Even now, ten years later, I can still relive that experience as if it happened yesterday. The culmination of these six months led to the crystallization of my life purpose, an aspirational statement that I knew was mine but, at the time, had no idea how it would manifest.

These magical months of coaching opened up a whole new world for me. In addition to my current life of work, family and responsibility, I now had this other parallel life of possibility, connection and deeper truth. At the time I remember having to hold these very carefully as two separate realities - an outer one and an inner one. All of these new discoveries about my true self were so precious and fragile that they remained safely guarded to the outside world. They needed nurturing and strengthening before I could even consider a cross-over into my "other" life.

Over the course of this coaching journey my true self started to shine brighter. I became more aware of the conditions that were creating the tensions in my life, whether it be at work, with friends or at home with the family. Most of it came down to not being able to reconcile the rational world I was operating in and the sensitive inner qualities I was in the process of recognizing and claiming for myself. My intuitive abilities were yearning to come through, but I could not find an effective channel for that in the corporate environment that valued data, logic and reason above all.

Also, at home I was struggling to see how I could be more of my true self with my wife who prided herself to be highly rational and a "genius with numbers". Whenever I started a sentence with "I feel..." I would be met with a confused and slightly uninterested look. So as a result, I kept most of that to myself, assuming that these two worlds - the world of the head and the world of the heart - had to be kept separate. Even my whole journey into coaching was not known to many people. It was too difficult to explain what it was and why I was doing it. Most of the calls I had with my West Coast coach were done late at night in the quiet and confidence of my car.

It didn't take long before living this separation started to take its toll. It wasn't that different than living a lie. More and more my outer life started to feel like one. I could not imagine a way forward in the long term without a significant upheaval on all fronts, including both work and the home front.

During this period of inner clarity and outer turmoil only a handful of people felt trusted enough to share my inner process. As I confided in them, I could feel the momentum to take action slowly build. The energy that was rising within me was that of a warrior. I was going to show myself to the world no matter the consequences. If it meant being fired from my job, so be it. If I was going to lose some people along the way, then that was a price I was willing to pay. I realize now that I was very much living in the either-or paradigm. Either I be true to myself and accept the consequences or I continue to suffer feeling disconnected with the world around me. Within all of this there was one nonnegotiable - the wellbeing of my wife and two children Oscar and Audrey who, at the time, were 4 and 2 years old.

I knew the next step of showing myself to the world was near. I also knew that significant change was on the horizon. I had no idea though what the new configuration would look like once the dust had settled. Under normal circumstances the fear of the unknown would have led to inertia but, fueled by this warrior energy, I was ready to move through it.

QUESTIONS FOR THE BEING ENTREPRENEUR:

- What aspects of yourself feel like a curse but deep down you know are a gift?

- What would it take to embrace all aspects of the self?

- What small steps can you take to start polishing and bring forth your hidden gift?

4. I'm in it and that's all I can see

We all have an inner world; a part of ourselves that is raw, delicate, and deeply personal. At the heart of that inner world lies our life purpose - often only felt as a silent whisper in those rare moments of deep connection with ourselves. This subtle knowingness of "why we are here" is perhaps the most precious gift we have, yet it is also the most fragile one. Therefore, the impulse to protect it, or even ignore it, is very natural. As Being Entrepreneurs, we are compelled to listen deeply to this inner calling and then, little by little, express it through our entrepreneurial initiatives into the world.

Having been coached, I learned a lot about myself but I also realized that this was an art that I naturally embodied throughout my life and now it was yearning to express itself in a more deliberate and professional way.

It didn't take long to identify the coaching school most aligned with my values and beliefs. What appealed to me most was the deep spiritual nature of the program. Rather than focus on enhancing the Doing - increase productivity, achieve goals, improve personal effectiveness - I was about to sign up for a coaching school with a clear focus on Being. I was going to learn how to put the Human Spirit, the yearning of the heart and the inner voice at the center of the coaching process. Over the next 12 months I would discover how this coaching methodology can reveal the unique calling, or life purpose, that lies within each one of us and support the re-building of our lives around it.

At the time I didn't quite realize how bold of a decision this was. I truly believed that after this program I would be equipped to bring this deep transformational coaching into organizations. At the time I dreamed of (re)-igniting the collective spirit of an organization. The particularities of how I would do that and whether or not people even wanted it seemed irrelevant at the time. I was discovering that this was my life purpose, my mission in life, and simply trusted that eventually everything would fall into place. Trying to plan it all out in advance was not going to work - this much I knew. The best I could do was take it one step at a time.

The first step was clear: a week in San Diego immersed in the 5-day in person part of the course. It was exhilarating to dive deeply into both the personal journey and the skills aspect of this learning experience. I was good at it and could see infinite ways to experiment with all these new skills on Monday morning when I returned to work. The rest of the 12 months course unfolded online. The timing of these webinars was 17:30 to 19:30 pacific standard time, which was 2:30 to

4:30 am for me in Europe. My love for this work was such that getting up in the middle of the night on a weekday was effortless and somehow infused me with so much positive energy that it easily sustained me at work the following day. In fact, there was no better way for the newly acquired coaching concepts to flow into my day-to-day activities.

My world was now coaching and that was all I could see (and do). The inner world that, until recently, was private and protected had been released. My passion was now visible to all and many people around me were intrigued. I was fortunate to have a very open-minded boss at the time. She not only admired my newfound passion, but she was also one of the people who intuitively understood the benefit of deeper personal work. So, when I proposed to facilitate a "discover your true self" session during an upcoming team off-site event, she agreed without fully knowing what it would entail.

It was a huge opportunity for me to take this group of 10 business colleagues through my newly acquired visualization exercise. This included a deep meditation guiding them to a point in time, five years in the future. There they would meet their future self who had grown into his or her greatest potential. In this deep meditative state, they could experience what it feels like to have grown into their future self, even asking him or her for guidance to take back into the present moment. After the 30-minute exercise we took quality time to share our experiences and, in the process, got to know each other, and our aspirations in life and work, in a much more intimate way. We had collectively crossed the boundaries of what it meant to be colleagues in a business environment. Having glimpsed into each other's souls we knew that our future working relationship would be impacted, but how was not yet clear. All we knew was that at the time it felt great and for me it was a major breakthrough in closing the gap between the two parallel lives I had been living.

I was ready for more. I could see the tremendous possibilities to impact the business by coaching people at the individual and collective level. In my mind all of the typical interpersonal challenges people experience in the business context could be resolved if only we spent a bit more time deeply listening to each other and looking at the challenges with fresh eyes. I also understood that any shift in perspective we have towards others must first start with a shift in our own thoughts and belief patterns. This was so obvious to me and I naively assumed it would be relatively easy for others to acknowledge as well. A new world had opened up for me so why couldn't it open up for all of us.

In my mind, coaching was clearly the solution to all of life's problems and I was perfectly positioned to support the business in this new capacity. So, while continuing to fulfill the requirements of my consumer research responsibilities, I became an active advocate for transformational coaching amongst my colleagues and anyone else who crossed my path at work. Clearly some people got it. They happened to be younger and generally struggling to find their place within this large, highly competitive organizational environment. They too were feeling a disconnect between the yearning of their heart - meaningful work in collaboration with people I like - and the reality of the current culture - race to the top.

So, I started to attract my first clients. As I was coaching them mainly during business hours there was of course no question of charging for it. For me it was simply a way to be of service and gain valuable coaching hours needed to complete my certification. I could start to see where this might go. If I could show enough impact with this new line of work, then surely it would catch the attention of management and eventually a new position of "in-house coach" would be created. I was on a path of creating my dream job.

This vision was so appealing that I started to give more and more energy to the people I was supporting. I was so invested in their reality that I could no longer distinguish between what was theirs to work through and what was mine. The boundaries of a healthy coaching relationship were blurring and, although at the time I was not really aware of it, I was starting to lose myself. I was carrying the weight of other people's problems and lost touch with my own needs.

My sleep was the first thing to get affected. I can remember spending many sleepless nights "playing around" in my mind with the challenges of the clients I was supporting. At first it would yield some great insights that I would excitedly share with them the next day. Although it felt I was supporting them, my insights were not their insights and therefore would rarely stick. In my effort to be a great coach, I had lost touch with the first rule of coaching: the client is infinitely resourceful. They will learn what they need to learn when they are ready to learn it. I cannot do the work for them.

Sleepless nights became a pattern and soon enough it started to impact my mood and concentration. At work I was barely able to meet the minimum job requirements and at home I was feeling disconnected with my young family. It was a very confusing time.

One client relationship in particular had gotten a hold of me. Not only did we share a deep connection, but she also worked for me. Coaching somebody under these circumstances is of course far from ideal. At first it was exciting to share in such a profound way but soon it became clear I was treading on dangerous waters. I was no longer in control of my rational self and my behavior became increasingly reckless. I didn't realize at the time, but I was under a sort of spell and some very strange and scary things started to happen to me.

One incident still gives me the chills when I think back on it. It happened on my drive back from work. I remember having had an intense conversation with this friend / client / colleague. We had reached the stage where I could no longer be the person she had gotten to know over the past months. Our relationship had transcended time and space. We knew each other's deepest thoughts, fears and aspirations. At this stage I was completely unprotected. All energies - good or bad ones - had unlimited access. I had lost touch with my boundaries and as a result with my sense of self.

So that evening on my drive back from work, all of a sudden, out of thin air, a car appeared in my lane driving at high speed directly towards me. In that instant I was looking death in the eyes. In that same instant, I was overcome with another force that took control of my body and miraculously helped me veer off into the other lane to avoid the imminent head on collision. All of this happened in a fraction of a second and when I looked in the rear-view mirror, I saw nothing. The black speeding car had vanished back into thin air. The only remaining proof that something had happened was the pounding of my heart.

That incident was my wake-up call. It was the gift I needed to see how far I had drifted from my own being. It was a slap in the face that brought me back to my senses. The spell I was under was losing its grip. However, this was only a part of the awakening process.

A few months later I was diagnosed with cancer. After the initial scare it didn't take long to start connecting the dots. The pain and shame of living this double life had accumulated to such an extent that now it was manifesting as a cancer. I knew that the medical procedure was only part of the healing process. The rest would have to happen at an energetic level.

The next few months felt like another layer of coming out. First it was my newfound passion for coaching and now I had to stand in my truth about this disease. What's interesting is that the source of the cancer was so clear to me that I never felt like a victim. Instead I quickly accepted that it was a natural physical reaction to the turbulent nature of my energetic state over the previous months. This was not a random assault on my health, and I was not an innocent bystander. Although unintentionally, I had created the conditions for this to happen.

Instead of beating myself up for it, I was able to channel this awareness into the healing process. With some people I could share all the parts of the unfolding story and with others I would simply talk about the disease as a teacher, bearing some valuable lessons at this stage of my life. Being able to speak so freely, and positively, about my cancer was empowering me. It was also the key to breaking the spell and re-grounding the foundation of my life. Within a few months I was back on my feet with the profound realization that as a coach, and highly sensitive person, I would need to get better at maintaining healthy boundaries with my clients.

Having learnt this lesson the hard way was perhaps the only way for me to avoid these kinds of messy coach/client relationships from repeating themselves in the future. For this I am grateful to all the people who walked this path with me. It has prepared me to commit even more fully to my purpose. The next step was now becoming clear.

QUESTIONS FOR THE BEING ENTREPRENEUR:

- Think of a time when you were fully committed to following your heart. What actions did you take? How did it feel?

- How did the people around you react? Did it lead to the expected outcome?

- What did you learn from the experience?

5. Departure

At some point a Being Entrepreneur must take the leap and move from an arm's length relationship with their vision to fully stepping into it and embodying it. In this rite of passage some parts of ourselves get left behind. Perhaps it's a job or relationship that we have outgrown. Or maybe it's a deeply held belief or thought pattern that no longer serves us. Shedding the comforts of who we have been, and fully embracing who we are becoming, makes room for the exciting adventures that lie ahead.

Somewhere around 2010, I was introduced to the idea of past lives. It was not such a far stretch for me to believe that our spirit or soul has had past incarnations and will continue to have them in the future as well. I was fascinated by the idea that connecting with my past life could give more context to the human experience I am having today.

What I discovered, working with a past life guide, was that I had been a soldier in the first or second world war. This person helped me remember a specific moment in time, on the battlefield, when I could have played an important role in brokering peace and reconciliation. At some level I knew I had the gift of opening hearts and creating space for understanding but I was overcome by fear and chose to remain in the background and not act in that critical moment in time.

Having had this vivid experience made me realize that our life purpose probably doesn't change much as we transition between lives. What changes is our readiness and willingness to fully step into it. What this experience taught me was that I had once again arrived at an important fork in the road.

Now was the time to lean in and fully commit to my purpose despite the overwhelming fear around the unknown. There was a profound awareness that if I didn't seize this opportunity now then it would simply come back knocking at my door, even more powerfully, at some point in the future.

At work it was clear that the freedom I had been given to experiment with transformational coaching on the fringes of my job would not translate into a dedicated position. The gap between my lofty ideas and the pragmatism of the organization was simply too big. To their credit, the HR leader did hear me out and genuinely attempted to understand what I had in mind. However, it seemed my future, for now at least, lied elsewhere. Not having been able to make it work internally, I was now sure that resigning from my 10-year corporate career was the right thing to do. I knew in my heart that I had come to that important fork in the road. I could feel a huge energy pulling me towards something new.

It was this energy that one day propelled me to blurt out: "I'm ready to move on" while having coffee with my boss. I had not planned to do this when I left home that morning, nor had I aligned this big decision with my family beforehand. At some level I knew that asking for my wife's support would have led to lengthy discussions about the pros and cons with the possibility of fear taking over. This was a decision coming from a deep knowing that I had to take on my own. So, when I came home that evening with the big news, it was of course met with resistance and fear. At this point my lofty ideas were even more out of touch with reality than they had appeared to the HR leaders within the company (at least they had a decent understanding of the coaching concept). My family was genuinely concerned that I had lost my way.

I understood the fear, and even anger, for not having included my wife in the decision making. All I could ask was for her to trust me and join me in believing that everything would work out. I'd use the next six months of transition time to craft my business plan and make my grand coaching ideas more concrete. Surely this would help to bring her on board.

Unknowingly at the time I was putting pressure on myself to prove to my family that this decision was not a mistake. The story in my head was shifting. Concrete results - clients, projects, revenue...- would need to come relatively soon. I needed a business plan. Soon enough I was doing all the same things I had been conditioned to do during my working career, expecting that meticulous planning would be the key ingredient for success. I was approaching the launch of my coaching practice as I would the launch of a new laundry detergent. In hindsight this seems comical but at the time this was all I knew. So the last six months before resigning were filled thinking about my target audience, USP, RTB, 4P's, etc....

I had contracted a designer for the logo and website. And I had a three-year roadmap that would bring me back to the same level of income as I had before leaving. Most importantly, I had an inspiring name I was going to stand behind. My coaching practice would be called: Inner Voice Calling. It was a bold statement beautifully capturing who I was as a person and what I thought the world needed at the time.

Businesses had lost touch with their essence, their soul. I could see myself helping them reconnect with that inner voice, listen to it and then from that inner place, unleash a new wave of creativity and innovation. If it had worked for me personally then why wouldn't it work for organizations struggling to find their way in these uncertain times. In my eyes it was a solid proposition. Even though the market wasn't explicitly asking for such a proposition, I could feel that the underlying need was there. Surely my enthusiasm and conviction could be the bridge between what the market needs and what they want.

I was on track for a January 1st, 2010 launch. What I didn't know at the time was that I had fallen victim to another spell. This time it wasn't the energies of my clients pulling me off track, it was the illusion of control and my fixation on short term success that had its grip on me.

Carl Jung once said: "The greatest burden a child must bear is the unlived life of its parents". Looking back now, it occurs to me that my actions were in part motivated by a sense of rebellion towards my father and grandfather, which brings me back to the beginning of this story. My father had wanted to pursue a life as an artist, but my grandfather encouraged him to go into business. Unconsciously this "play it safe" approach to life was also passed on to me.

Therefore, breaking away from this pattern came with a great sense of responsibility. The burden of proof that another way was possible was now lying with me. If I could make it happen then the future of my kids and the generations afterwards would also be free to live the life of their dreams.

So, beneath the surface, well beyond my awareness at the time, a lot was at play. These intergenerational dynamics were adding to the pressure I was feeling to manifest my new business and successfully prove that the big ideas about organizational transformation would soon translate into concrete projects. This "spell" would on the one hand fuel great creativity and on the other hand lead to defensive behavior. Since failure, or changing course, was not an option, I found myself in a place of needing approval and positive acknowledgments more than I usually would. Constructive feedback, or criticism, of Inner Voice Calling and the approach I was taking was met with resistance. I had convinced myself that having the support from close friends and family was critical to the success of this endeavor. Once again, I had given my power away.

Despite all of the pressure I was putting on myself, I gave it my best shot. The first six months of Being Entrepreneurship were solely focused on getting my first clients. I had reached out to all my contacts and, given the good personal relationship I had built up with them over the years, they often gave me the opportunity to present my new business and explore ways in which I could support them. My passion, courage and conviction came through most of the time. Prospects would acknowledge and admire this but at the end of the day there was nothing they could do for me. The ideas were simply too far removed from their stated priorities that they couldn't find a way to bring me in, even if they wanted to.

At the same time many of my old colleagues were observing from a distance, skeptical but curious to see if I would be able to pull this off. Every time I was asked how things were going, I had to put on a brave face and dig deep inside to keep my energy strong. I had a few coaching clients but none of them really bought into Inner Voice Calling. They simply trusted me as a person.

On one occasion I remember a client carefully asking me if I could invoice them as an independent coach rather than through my company name. Although they didn't explicitly say so, I suspect it had to do with them not feeling comfortable handing over an Inner Voice Calling invoice to their finance department.

It didn't take long before my own inner voice started to feel shaky. Answering the "how are things going" question became more and more difficult. My confidence dropped and from there it didn't take long to reach my breaking point.

In parallel to the slow start of my new business I was also finding my way in this new role as a stay-at-home dad. I hadn't expected that stripping away my well-respected corporate persona would have such a profound effect on my sense of self-worth. I imagined the neighbors or parents from my kid's school wondering to themselves if I had lost my job or if I was suffering from a burnout. Their perceived pity seemed to only increase when I hesitantly told them about my "exciting" new business venture.

So, while doors were closing on the business front, I was also feeling isolated at home. Spending more time with the kids was my greatest source of joy. Perhaps better than anyone, they could feel the significance and importance of the steps I was taking. They were also genuinely curious about the new path I was walking on.

I remember one day my 5-year-old son asking me what "coaching" is. It was great getting that question from him as it forced me to strip down this idea to its essence. I told him it was about helping people discover what they love doing and then building their life around that. He was silent for a while and then, innocently asked: "How can a coach know what other people love doing"? It was such a simple, yet profound, observation which further opened up the conversation.

I went on to say that the beauty of coaching is that the coach doesn't need to know what is right for the other person. They simply need to believe, and deeply trust, that we all already have the answers inside of us. The idea that a coach holds space and asks questions rather than advises or mentors resonated deeply with my five-year-old son. He intuitively understood this new paradigm of learning that was still so foreign to most people. These were the precious moments that fueled me with new energy and inspiration.

Having so much quality time with my 3-year-old daughter and 5-year-old son was incredibly rewarding and a real contrast to the way it was when I was still in a 9-5 job. During that time, my wife and I would drop the kids off at day-care around 7:30am and pick them up at 18:30pm, 5 days per week. The evenings were hectic. We needed to prepare dinner, get the kids ready for bed and then hop back on to our laptops to complete unfinished work from the office. The little time we had together in the evening was far from enjoyable. There was no time to switch off and become present for each other. Instead, the fatigue of the long day often led to arguments.

It was also the weight of this dysfunctional family life that eventually pushed me to resign. What I didn't yet fully comprehend at the time was how much joy and inspiration I would get from being a stay-at-home dad. The kids made me feel fully alive again. Even though the new business was floundering, I could feel my creative juices coming back. The following poem, which I wrote on my daughter's first day of school, is an example of that.

September 4th, 2012

To my daughter on her first day of school:

Go learn to read and write
But keep your dreams in sight
When told what is wrong and right
Listen to your inner light
If at times you feel incomplete
Focus on what makes you unique

May innocence and wonder
Guide you through the thunder
And reveal the truths down under

Back in the quiet of the home
I feel somewhat alone
It's like the first day for me too
I ponder what to do

Are my dreams in sight?
Can I listen to my inner light?

You inspire me to try
Make it impossible to lie
You give me hope
To climb this slippery slope

Your smile warms my heart
I am ready to restart

The steps I had taken to follow my purpose were great, but I was starting to realize that they were just the very first steps of a much longer journey. It was naive for me to think that such an ambitious career / life change would come with short term impact. However, it wasn't surprising. In my mind, it felt like I had already travelled such a long way. The coaching school had been a 12 months investment, leaving a well-paying job was a momentous move and creating a new business proposition all felt like a lifetime's work, even though it had only been two years. It wasn't easy to gain this perspective and acknowledge that all the hard work and turmoil I had experienced in the last years was only a fraction of what lay ahead.

Six months into my entrepreneurial venture, I hit a wall. Keep on doing the same things, expecting different results was no longer possible. Something foundational needed to change but I had no idea what that was. All I knew was that going back to a corporate job or even positioning myself as a freelance market researcher was not an option.

This inner tension built up until one day, in the middle of a sleepless night, I got up at 3am, walked out into the woods and screamed. I didn't stop until all the pain, anger, resentment, self-pity and frustration was released.

When I woke up the next morning, everything was different. I felt lighter, freer, something had shifted deep inside. Although the neighbors may not have heard me, the Universe certainly did. It effortlessly received the burden I was carrying and in doing so I could surrender, let go and re-start my journey from a place of greater innocence and trust.

QUESTIONS FOR THE BEING ENTREPRENEUR:

- Where in your life, or on your entrepreneurial journey, do you feel stuck?

- When you take a step back, do you recognize old patterns sabotaging the steps you are taking to create something new in your life?

- What would it take to fully surrender and release all the built-up tension?

6. Transformation & apprenticeship

When a Being Entrepreneur gets stuck, which inevitably will happen, it may seem like there are only two options: push harder or let go of the dream. In these moments of frustration, we are being invited to step into the "third way". However, accessing this new realm of possibility, first requires a change in our BEING.

In my case this meant letting go of the belief that 1) I knew what my prospective clients needed and 2) I was already prepared to serve them in this way. By surrendering into "not knowing" I gave myself permission to become an explorer again. I could now engage people in meaningful dialogue about their aspirations and pain points (rather than feel the pressure to persuade them about my proposition).

Off-loading the burden, I was carrying until then helped me see beyond the self-imposed constraints I had put on myself and the business. The short term results I had been expecting were simply unrealistic given the magnitude of the vision I was holding. From this new place I could sense another way forward. I was being invited to let go of outcomes, time constraints and, most importantly perhaps, the belief that I was READY to fully embrace and deliver transformational coaching in organizations.

This was the moment to fundamentally re-define success from something that is outside of my control (projects, sales, clients, profit...) to something I can fully embrace irrespective of the circumstances. This simple shift in perspective was incredibly liberating. I was starting to surrender into a more trusting partnership with the "universal forces". As long as I continue to focus on projects that are a pure expression of my authentic self AND within my control, then the universe will do its part to open doors and show me the next steps on the path.

The first idea that came to me as a result of stepping into this alternate paradigm of entrepreneurship was very simple, but also very profound. What if I didn't know what organizations needed? What if, instead of closing the previous market researcher chapter, I would reclaim it and build on it in this new chapter?

Sure enough, one day, shortly after opening myself up to these new possibilities, I knew in every cell of my body what I needed to do next. It was so obvious now yet only a few weeks ago it would have been impossible to imagine.

During the next 6 - 12 months I would put on hold everything I thought I knew about organizational transformation and re-immerse into this field as a researcher to genuinely explore what it takes to bring a new level of consciousness into organizations. I imagined creating a short documentary film in which I interview a wide range of thought leaders and weave together a compelling story that would give more context and inspiration for the deep transformational work I aspire to do with leaders and their organizations. It would be a rite of passage of sorts, one that would not only be a rich source of insights, but also serve to build my credibility as a thought leader & storyteller of the new paradigm.

It was hugely ambitious, especially because I had very limited filmmaking experience, but it was one that was within my control. So, I started putting together a plan. At least 5 or 6 visionary leaders came to mind that I had worked with and would be open to such an interview. I could also think of a couple of spiritual mentors who could beautifully speak about the awakening that is happening in society and the evolutionary impact this is having on all our systems and structures. The plan also consisted of a budget, timeline and overall theme that would tie everything together. Specifically, I wanted to know what it meant to bring HEART into business. Here's an extract of the plan that had come together (I even had a logo designed to represent the questioning / exploring nature of the initiative).

THE BEING ENTREPRENEUR

What is it about?

Operation Heart in Business is a documentary that explores / investigates the role of Heart in business. It takes something which in many ways is misunderstood or even taboo in the business environment and demonstrates how in fact operating from the Heart is the single most important breakthrough any business can make. The film aims to touch the Heart of organizational leaders and inspire them to step up to the exciting possibilities that exist when the Heart gets a bigger place at the corporate decision-making table. The story unfolds from the perspective of four different stakeholders:

1. The young generation entering the workforce with high ideals and an intense desire to make a difference
2. Experienced business leaders who have concrete examples to share on how the heart has opened up exciting new possibilities
3. Coaches & facilitators who can objectively see the transformation that is taking place
4. "Experts of the Heart" who can speak to the vast possibilities that exist when we operate from this place.

How will it come together?

1. **Interviews & content generation**: the following people from my network have offered to share their stories on how the Heart manifests in the workplace, how it impacts business performance and what transformation needs to take place for it to become a central part of an organizations' culture

Stakeholder	Candidate	Credentials	Availability
Business students /	Short, spontaneous interviews at	Leaders of tomorrow, bring fresh ideas and	No pre-screening, anyone

recent graduates	universities or with young managers on their way to and from work (intercepts on the bus/underground)	aspirations into the workplace	who is willing to share their thoughts on the topic for a couple of minutes
Experienced leaders (all have personally volunteered to participate & have great stories to share)	Till Wahnbaeck Peter Yorke Virginie Helias Nuno Bernardo Laurent Rochat Kate Barker Robert Torrance Omar Mahmoud Axialent client	Sales Director Wella Germany Global Marketing Director Pampers Marketing Director P&G GM P&G South East Africa Founder Innovation Atelier Global Brand Manager BBC Earth VP Sales Ethical Investments Market Knowledge Director	Confirmed Confirmed Confirmed Confirmed Confirmed Confirmed Confirmed Waiting response Waiting response
Coaches, facilitators, consultants	David Robinson Alice Larsen Sujith Ravindran	Founder The Circle Project	Confirmed Confirmed Confirmed

	Mark Silver	Founder New Day Company Founder Being at Full Potential Founder, Heart of Business	Confirmed
Experts of the Heart	Alan Seale	Founder, Center for Transformational Presence	Confirmed
	HeartMath Institute	Leading research on the intelligence of the Heart	Confirmed

2. Timeline:

Complete Project	Start Date	End Date
	01/01/2011	31/10/2011
Planning	01/01/2011	31/05/2011
Concept design	01/01/2011	31/03/2011
Recruitment & funding	01/04/2011	15/05/2011
Interview Preparation	16/05/2011	31/05/2011
Fieldwork	01/06/2011	20/07/2011
Geneva interviews	01/06/2011	31/06/2011
UK interviews	18/06/2011	20/06/2011
Germany interview	25/06/2011	27/06/2011
US interviews	03/07/2011	17/07/2011
Brussels interview	18/07/2011	20/07/2011
Analysis & production	01/08/2011	31/10/2011
Analysis & storyline development	01/08/2011	15/08/2011
Editing & production	16/08/2011	31/08/2011
Review & alignment with key stakeholders	01/09/2011	30/09/2011
Deployment & launch	01/10/2011	31/10/2011

I was curious why highly respected business leaders like Steve Jobs or hard core physicists like Albert Einstein, who had come to the conclusion that Heart or the Inner Voice were key to their success, were not having more impact on the way we run our organizations.

"Don't let the noise of other's opinions drown out your own inner voice. And most important, have the courage to follow your heart and intuition. They somehow

already know what you truly want to become. Everything else is secondary." Steve Jobs

"Everyone who is seriously involved in the pursuit of science becomes convinced that a spirit is manifest in the laws of the universe, a spirit vastly superior to man." Albert Einstein

On the one hand we recognize these deep universal truths and on the other hand we discard them as impractical when it comes to day-to-day management. This was a fascinating paradox that I was determined to shine light on in my research project.

So, I went ahead and bought myself a small handheld camera and reached out with my idea to the people I wanted to interview. It was beautiful how quickly and positively people got back to me. Such a contrast to the painful experience of "selling" my services until then. I was finding it so much easier to engage people from this open place of discovery and genuine curiosity. There was energy in the idea and before long a plan had come together that would take me to Vancouver, Seattle, San Francisco, Boston and then back to Europe. It was exhilarating to be moving forward on my entrepreneurial journey with such purpose, freedom and commitment. I guess the Universe also liked what was unfolding because one day, out of the blue, I received an email from Lia Jaspers.

Lia is somebody I met a couple of years earlier while doing market research on laundry detergents in Munich. It was one of the most magical days of my market research career. I was scheduled to spend a full day with Lia to understand how doing the laundry, and her choice of products, fit into the broader context of her life. This ethnographic research was the most powerful way to extract mind and heart opening insights. Not only because it was easier to connect the dots between who somebody is as a person and their laundry habits and practices, but also because spending a whole day with someone made it possible to establish a deeper, trusting connection. They would share more freely and, as a result, deeper insights got revealed.

In my case, I got a little distracted from the laundry detergent learning objectives when Lia started talking about her life as a documentary filmmaker. She was an adventurous spirit who fearlessly travelled around the world to capture the important, but often under-reported, human stories. There was purpose and passion in everything she did. She inspired me to also open up and share my emerging ideas about the evolving paradigm in organizations and how I was starting to see a role for me to play in facilitating this transition. Together we imagined the possibility of a documentary film that would reveal the need for profound organizational transformation through the lens of the more conscious, younger generation entering the workforce. It was exciting to dream about these possibilities but at the end of the day I was still a market researcher for laundry detergents so the prospects of making it happen was unrealistic at the time.

Upon my return home, I wrote Lia a postcard thanking her for the inspiring day and left my email address, hoping we could stay in touch. Apart from the postcard she wrote back to me, we didn't hear from each other until 2 or 3 years later - when all the stars were aligned.

In her email Lia spoke about finding the postcard I had sent after our day together in Munich, remembering our talk about the evolving business world and googling to see what I was up to. She found Inner Voice Calling website and was so pleased to see the changes I had made that she felt compelled to reach out and playfully ask what had become of my documentary idea. Of course, she didn't know that I was planning the heart in business film adventure so receiving her message in that moment was even more mind blowing to me. It was from this point on that my trust in universal forces really started to become a way of life.

A couple of skype calls later, I had not one, but two professional documentary filmmakers join me on my adventures. Normally this would of course never have been possible with the small budget I had put aside but the project, and the North America road trip that came with it, was so inspiring to them that they agreed to join me. I simply needed to cover their travel and accommodation costs.

Here's a note from my journal that I wrote just before boarding the plane and starting this journey.

As I board the plane, kicking off a two-week road trip to the US, I feel the same as I did many years ago when I went to visit an old girlfriend in Arizona. At the time I remember being on a mission. I talked about it as something I needed to do but didn't yet know what it was. Deep inside I was being called to reconnect with this person who taught me how to love, but I had no expectations of re-discovering the magic we once had.

Many people supported my quest in beautiful ways, as if they could relate, or wished they had done something similar. And somehow, I was totally OK with those who thought I was crazy or just needed to move on. The trip was filled with precious moments – happy ones, painful ones and sad ones. I experienced them all as fully as I could and on the last day, late at night, everything became clear.

There was something important I needed to say, something that was hiding deep inside my heart and finally at that moment I was able to access and express the feeling that was holding me back. I discovered a deep inner peace, said goodbye and opened up the space to love once again.

As I board the plane, kicking off a two week road trip to the US, I can't help but wonder if my quest to uncover the Heart in Business will also come with many deep personal gifts like the ones I experienced when I followed my heart to Arizona.

There are certainly many questions whirling around inside of me: is the business world ready for more heart, is it possible to make the heart more tangible and relevant to business, will I be able to create shifts in perspective, is there room for the deep transformational work I want to do in organizations, can I be successful in my new career path? Wow, despite my bright hopes and dreams of a more heart-centered business world, there are many doubts and fears lurking around the corner.

When I committed to my calling one and a half years ago, I knew it would be challenging but I felt well equipped and trusted that the right opportunities would present themselves. Looking back now I am definitely grateful for the very interesting projects that have come my way but somehow I have not yet attracted the deeper transformational work that I believe can have such a powerful impact in the business context.

Have I not positioned myself in the right way? Am I not connecting with the needs? Do I need to build more credibility and trust, or is the timing just not right? Can I trust my own heart which is clearly telling me to continue down this road or do I give into the fear and settle back into a more secure life? I am clearly at a crossroads…

As I board the plane, kicking off a two-week road trip to the US, I know some powerful discoveries are about to happen. I will walk away wiser and have an incredible story to tell. Some of the questions will be answered, others will fade away, and I suspect new ones will arise. Perhaps this is what it's all about: staying open, discovering the gifts and trusting that in this flow I will get in touch with the greatest potential that wants to emerge.

Upon our return, I was handed a hard drive with 100+ hours of footage to sort through and create an overall storyline no longer than 10 - 12 minutes long. At first it was a daunting task. I didn't know where to start and had no prior experience. It took me a couple of months of dedicated work to bring this wealth of wisdom down to its essence. In doing so, not only did I discover the art of editing, but I also processed and integrated the insights from the various interviews at a deeper level within my own being. This felt like the rite of passage I needed to go through before I could engage business leaders in a credible way.

At the end of these months an overall narrative emerged that would naturally tie the essential content pieces together. I reached out to Lia, flew to Munich, and within a couple of days, the film I had dreamt up 12 months ago, had become a reality.

I now had an inspiring story to tell. In the process of collecting insights from experts about the value of more heart in business, I had become a credible expert myself. This was not just a theoretical piece of work. It became the foundation of how I show up in my own business. Fully embodying the heart in business principles would become the most compelling way to engage others and eventually earn the trust of clients.

At the core of this approach was a radical redefinition of success. Until then, I had thought about it as a function of the output I achieved. This traditional approach made me focus on things mostly out of my control (for example, signing up clients, yearly revenue targets…). As a result of the heart in business project I altered my relationship with success. Instead of defining it as the quantity of business generated, it was now all about the quality of conversations I would have with anyone who came on my path. The beauty of defining success in this way is that it was now fully in my control. I could simply choose to tell my story and share my heart in business research findings with all the passion and excitement that I was feeling.

In doing so, some amazing things happened. Shifting the focus from selling to storytelling and authentically living my vision for a more heart-centered business sparked the curiosity, intrigue and eventually trust of the people I wanted to serve. Ironically, by letting go of outcomes, the outcomes I had been attached to previously, started to come. I was now attracting clients rather than selling to clients. This radically new way of doing business was not only more effective but also more fun and fulfilling. It also unleashed many more creative projects aimed at bridging the divide between where the business world is today and where it could be in the future.

The first one was a short story that unfolds as a dialogue between the voice of Business (representing the mainstream ideas about what business is or should be), the voice of what it could be (represented by Spirit or Potential), and my own voice as coach at the time. I started writing it as an experiment, curious what would happen when I authentically embodied both of these perspectives without judgment or bias.

The following interaction between myself and Spirit gives a sense of what I, and many other Being Entrepreneurs, will experience along the way.

Mark:
I am having one of those days when I am finding it difficult to see the bigger picture. It's as if I've fallen from the sky and landed back in a place of survival and fear. I can only see a few meters ahead of me. My dreams appear out of touch and impractical. I wonder if it is time to let go and move back into a more secure and predictable place. I am stuck in no man's land with one foot in a life full of hope, and another wanting to step back into a more conventional life. Has my time run out? Have I failed to demonstrate success in my new career path? Do I need to make a choice, or can I live happily somewhere in between? I have given the best of myself and am very proud of the effort I have put in. I will not look back on these years with regret, wishing I had done something different. I am wondering about the partnership with Spirit though. Although I have lots of evidence that this partnership can work, right now I feel alone and abandoned. I am doubting my ability to hold on to the dream, to keep taking steps in the right direction. I know the feeling is temporary and that breakthrough might be just around the corner but what I am experiencing is real and I want to live it as fully as possible. Right now that means being vulnerable, experiencing the pain and facing the fear. It's only in this openness that I can receive the gift. I wonder what it is…

Spirit:
I've been knocking on many doors these days, whispering words of encouragement and hope as more and more people are feeling the urgency to change. I am so excited about the shift that is taking place and the amount of people stepping into their true power. Every day I

am getting more requests to serve and contribute in a more meaningful way. Each time somebody steps up to the challenge and into the unknown they empower me to guide them along the way. It becomes so much easier for me to open doors, facilitate "chance" meeting and inspire new ideas. My wish is that our journeys into the unknown are as smooth and graceful as possible, but I realize it is not always easy to experience them as such. To welcome new ideas, we must first let go of the old ones. Just as some doors need to close before new ones can open. I am aware this process is painful and can take time. It requires inner work, openness, trust and patience. We can often feel alone and be tempted to turn around. I hear Mark's cry for help. I wish I could make it easier for him at the moment but there is only so much I can do. He needs time to process and extract the gifts from this experience. All I can say is doors are waiting to be opened.

Building on this approach of embodying the thoughts, feelings and fears of business leaders I aspired to serve, a next film project was born. I wanted to tell the story of a CEO the night before having to give an important speech to his organization. He is struggling to find a way in which he can share the disappointing business results while inspiring and motivating his people to move forward with next hope for the future. Rather than figuring out his speech in the office, he steps out into the night and has a series of "chance" encounters that significantly impact the way he perceives the challenges and decides to address the organization the next morning. When my filmmaking friends came back on board for this project, they encouraged me to take the embodiment experiment to a new level. I was not only the author of the story, I had also become the main actor, playing the role of the CEO.

The story unfolded as follows:

CEO talking to himself the night before an important speech to his organization:

It's late & I just got the final numbers in for the quarter. Once again, we have underperformed. It's now the 4th quarter in a row of declining sales. None of the strategic changes we have made over the last year seem to be working. Tomorrow morning, I need to announce the results to my organization, and then afterwards to the analysts on Wall Street. I have no idea what I am going to say. I've been telling them that conditions are improving and that our recent product upgrades and pricing interventions will put us back on track. We have even implemented a number of internal processes to boost productivity. I no longer believe this is working and I suspect the rest of the organization feels the same. This story is not working anymore but I have no idea where to go from here.

It's already 9pm, I'm starving. This will definitely be a long night, so I better get a quick bite to eat at the Chinese around the corner. Hopefully some inspiration will come.

Three hours later, I just got back into the office. What was supposed to be a quick bite turned into an incredible experience. It started with the fortune cookie I got at the end of my meal, which said: "The answers to your questions will be found in unexpected places". I wasn't sure what to make of this but somehow it resonated with me. So rather than going straight back to the office, which I normally would do, I wandered down the empty street. It was an unusually quiet night. All I could hear was a street performer playing his guitar in the background. It sounded nice so I walked over to listen in more carefully. He greeted me with a warm smile. His music was soothing and during those few moments all my worries about my speech disappeared. I thanked him and as I went to put some money in his case, I noticed a small sign lying beside it saying: "I warm Hearts. Who do you choose to be"? At this point the office was the last thing on my mind. Something was happening and I was curious what was in store for me next. It was time for a drink.

So, I ventured into the little café that I must have walked by many times before but never really noticed until now. I took a seat at the bar and ordered a pint of Sam Adams. I took out my fortune cookie message and laid it down beside my glass. There I was, a few hours before addressing my organization. I still had no idea what I was going to say but at this point I knew the answers would not be found in the office. I also knew I would have to look deep inside and question the kind of leader I had been and who I would choose to be in the future.

"Who do I choose to be"? That is a question I hadn't asked myself for a long while! As I took my first sip of Sam Adams, I was instantly transported back to my university years when I had spent some time in Boston. It reminded me of the energy and passion I once felt about making a difference in the world. Everything seemed possible. What has happened since then? I somehow forgot why I got into business in the first place. Had I slowly drifted away from who I was back then? Was now the time to re-connect?

At that moment one of our recent hires in the accounting department walked in and took a seat beside me. I had seen him before in the office, but we hadn't met officially yet. I was a bit embarrassed when he came to sit beside me because I didn't know his name. Luckily, he introduced himself and we got on talking. I asked him about the job and his first impressions of the company. It was so interesting to get a fresh perspective. His understanding of the business was impressive and to my surprise the story he saw in the numbers was very different from mine. I had been looking at the aggregated numbers and from this viewpoint things were obviously very bleak. But at a micro level he was seeing pockets of opportunity. Some of our efforts were actually working very well but they were small and got lost in the busyness of trying to fix the big problems. We've stopped seeing the parts of our business that are working!!

Of course, I wanted to know more. So, he went on to explain that the pockets of opportunity were coming from some of the "side projects" that were low on the strategic priority list but high on some people's passion list. In fact, one of the projects he mentioned I remember specifically asking the person to STOP working on it. I wonder how much bigger it could have been had I given him the green light and wholeheartedly supported the effort. I knew from now on I would have to start finding out.

My night back in the office turned out to be a very inspiring one. I even managed to get a few hours of sleep. A couple of minutes from now I will be giving my speech. It's going to be very different from the usual ones but for the first time in a long time I feel we are about to embark on an exciting new path, one that will truly re-energize our people and the business.

Good morning everyone, it's nice to see you all. Until a few hours ago I was dreading this talk because once again the overall numbers have not come in as expected. But some amazing things happened last night that have profoundly changed the way I look at the business and what I think we need to do to move forward. So rather than focus on our current results, I would like to take this time to share with you how my perspective has changed and the impact this will have on our organization.

My preparation for today's speech was very unusual. It was inspired by a fortune cookie, a street performer and finally a conversation with one of our colleagues, whom I bumped into while having a drink. It was this last conversation that helped me understand the biggest issue we are facing. I realized that our business is evolving and that my focus has been in the wrong place. In prioritizing the strategies that have worked for us in the past, I have not been able to see the new opportunities emerging in the marketplace. But many of you have and the initiative you took to develop these new ideas anyway seems to be paying out. A closer look at the data actually shows that, despite the overall decline in the numbers, there are some very promising pockets of opportunity. When I found out about this I was so moved by the passion and determination that so many of you bring to the job. I was also embarrassed that I hadn't been paying more attention to these efforts and supporting them in the right way.

Going forward this is going to change. I want to know about all the ideas bubbling up within the organization. I want us to harness the energy and passion in each one of you and use this to create projects that will once again put us at the leading edge of the industry. We will be replacing the tight controls we put in place to squeeze out more productivity with a more open & trusting culture to promote more creativity and responsibility. These changes are effective immediately!

The second insight I got from last night will be key in making these changes a reality. While watching the street performer I was prompted to think about a question that I hadn't considered for a long time. "Who do I choose to be"? Such a simple and powerful question but unfortunately it is one that I have ignored (perhaps because I have been too focused on the question: what do we choose to do?). It reminded me of the aspirations I had as a young business student. I was full of hope about the future and committed to making a meaningful difference in the world. Personally, I will be reflecting on this question but I would also like to encourage us to take some time and think about who we want to be as an organization? For example, what would our work be like if we chose to listen more deeply to each other, to ask the difficult questions and meet challenges with an open mind, to challenge the status quo, to encourage new ideas, to be passionate & creative…What would it take to commit to this new way of being?

Finally, we need to get out of the office more often. After my experience last night, I am convinced that there is so much valuable knowledge out there that is simply not available to us when we spend most of our time in the office. It's not just about spending more time with our customers and suppliers. We also need to think about how we interact with them and who we interact with (are we asking the right questions & listening deeply enough?). We need to pay more attention to our other stakeholders and understand how these relationships can be nurtured. We can look even beyond our stakeholders for inspiration. For example, in my case last night following the advice of a fortune cookie opened up a whole new set of experiences that ultimately led to the creation of this speech.

I sincerely believe that these changes are going to set us up for success in the long run. But it won't be easy, nor will it come overnight. The pressure to continue delivering short term results will not go away and we will need to do a better job of managing the expectations of Wall Street. Again, it is about how we choose to respond to these pressures and the story we decide to tell that will make the difference. I am convinced there are some big ideas coming to life in our organization and that we have incredibly talented and passionate people to make them happen. As long as we keep highlighting and drawing attention to this, I am sure our stakeholders will eventually come back on board too.

To conclude this chapter, I leave you with a poem I werote back then. It perfectly expresses the depth of personal transformation I was going through as part of my apprenticeship of becoming an important voice for the future of business.

The great divide:

On the left there is business
It loves to think, and problem solve
Move fast and talk with resolve
Perform so hard it wears you down
If only it would stop to breathe and look around

On the right there is Heart
Gently offering to play its part
It looks around from 10ft above
And knows deep inside
The time has come to think out wide
But this seed of possibility
Dream of a new reality
Will wither away on its own
If it sits there all alone

These worlds seem so far away
Many think they don't belong
But like a lover gone astray
Who says that with the right song
They won't come out to play?

More than ever they need each other

One to listen and one to talk
One to pause and one to walk
One to dream and one to act

THE BEING ENTREPRENEUR

One to trust and one with facts
One to flow and one to plan
One to focus and one to expand
One to think and one to feel
One to stretch and one to heal
One to sense and one to see
One to Do and one to Be

Together they are whole
Like partnering the Ego and the Soul

Deep inside my Heart
I feel I have a role to play
In uniting these worlds so apart
Help them see a way

But where do I start?
I'm tired going it alone
Do you feel the same
Out there on your own?

Together we can heal, make it real
We can hold hands, reach out, build bridges
And when new perspectives are revealed
Like with a masterpiece of art
Our minds will open
To business with a Heart

QUESTIONS FOR THE BEING ENTREPRENEUR:

- How have you defined success for your entrepreneurial project in the past?

- How can you shift the way you think about success so that it is no longer dependent on the outside world?

- What rite of passage do you need to experience before new inspiration can start coming through?

7. All the dots connect

What does giving birth have in common with BEING Entrepreneurship? Both require a significant period of gestation. A period of time where most of the work happens beneath the surface, at the level of our inner being. It will feel like there isn't much to show for your efforts, however, in reality, you are simply getting ready for an incredible outpouring of creativity and inspired manifestation!

The film and writing projects were all part of my apprenticeship. They were effective at generating curiosity and intrigue but there was still a way to go in turning this research into a tangible proposition that mainstream organizations could say "yes" to.

My last boss during my corporate career was somebody who deeply understood my ambitions and remained a friend after I left. Every once in a while, we would meet for coffee and share updates. As a highly respected leader in the organization, and somebody who had a great overview of the development needs internally, she was always sensing whether or not there was an opportunity to bring me back in as a coach or consultant. For me it was a great gauge to see how far, or close, my work was from the needs of the business. After every meeting I would walk away feeling encouraged with the progress but also with a new insight on how I could get one step closer to bring my services back into my old workplace.

I remember one meeting in particular where I had come to present the overall findings of my Heart in Business project. She not only loved the insights but also how I had gone back to my researcher roots. It was in that conversation that she encouraged me to look at what it would take to build on this qualitative research and create a quantitative measure of how much "Heart" was being expressed in an organization. We referred to it as the "Heart Quotient". I loved the idea and immediately knew that this would eventually be the bridge to making this work more accessible to organizations.

Quantifying Heart may sound like an oxymoron. Afterall, how can something so subjective be measured? Is it crazy to imagine that one day it could become the new metric for organizations to track and evaluate themselves on?

Common sense would suggest it is not possible but in that particular moment in time I knew it would be the next step on my Being

Entrepreneur journey. Afterall I had spent 10 years perfecting the art of quantifying and validating consumer insights during my researcher career. Why could I not apply these same skills to help bring more objectivity to the subjective nature of Heart (in Business)? Could it be that all my past experiences had set me up for this moment in time? I was up for the challenge, and I was not the only one!

My good friend, Sujith Ravindran, who I met during the late 90's during our MBA studies had been walking a parallel path over the past years. After graduating, he also joined the ranks of a large multinational corporation, became disillusioned and went on his personal transformation journey. For him this meant reconnecting and reclaiming his spiritual roots. As a child growing up with Guru's in India, he was a student of the rich mystical traditions, but over the years this wisdom had taken a back seat as it seemed incompatible with the demands of his modern life. It was during our many late-night chats that his rich mystical essence could freely shine through. In these enlightened moments I remember having many fascinating conversations about infusing corporate life with more depth and meaning. Although we weren't ready for it yet, we could both sense that one day we would create a business around these ideas.

I remember a crucial moment, as we were wrapping up our corporate careers, when we had to acknowledge that the time to join forces had not yet come. The idea of co-creating with such a good friend was compelling. However, we had to accept that, despite the similarities in the vision that we held, there were also important differences. Sujith's calling was to support individuals in their personal growth while I was passionate about working with organizations. At the time we could not reconcile the two and therefore concluded that it was best to walk our separate paths. Accepting that I first had to walk on my own was scary. It was not the comfortable choice but definitely turned out to be the right one at the time.

So, while I was researching Heart in Business, and learning my lessons on how to effectively bridge this work with organizations, Sujith was writing books and offering his talks and seminars. We continued to nurture our friendship and follow each other's adventures until one day, several years later, the "Heart Quotient" idea came up. This was the spark we had been waiting for. We instantly knew that the moment had come for our paths to converge. Creating a measurement tool that reveals the deeper essence of an organization was a huge challenge, but now we were ready to take it on.

What followed was six months of profound co-creation. We spent almost every evening on Skype sourcing the characteristics of a "Heart-centered" organization. We drew on the Heart in Business research, Sujith's extensive knowledge of the Indian mystical traditions as well as our personal experiences in the corporate world. We downloaded as much as we could without feeling rushed to structure and organize what was coming through us. Eventually a beautiful canvas of concepts and ideas had emerged.

With this extensive brainstorm in place, we could start to see some natural clusters starting to form. As we continued to play with all of this material, an overall framework appeared. It was in the shape of a house with each pillar being one of the clusters.

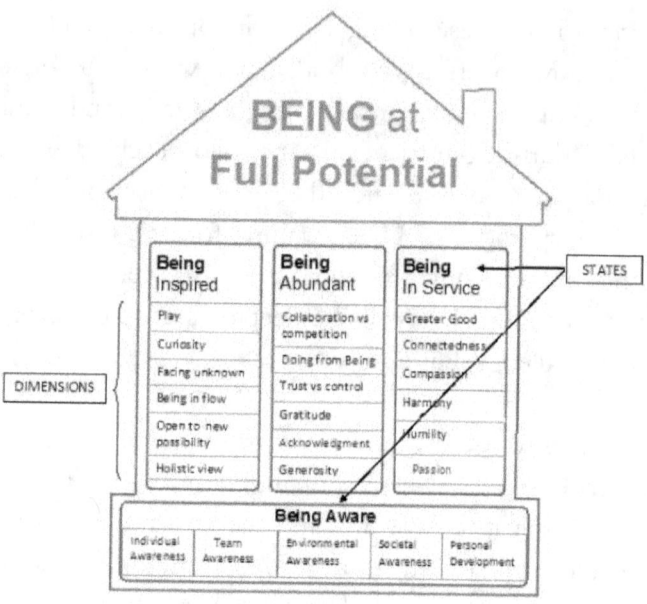

Now that we knew how to break this big fuzzy idea of Heart in Business down into more specific dimensions, we could start the next phase of our co-creative process. This involved developing the questionnaire of the Heart Quotient survey. After several more weeks we ended up with a list of 83 questions. Some of them spoke directly to our rational mind and others took us to a more intuitive place where we had to imagine how we would behave in certain situations.

Example of question speaking to rational mind	Example of questions speaking to our intuition
I have clarity on my principles and values	Which of the following statements best describes how you deal with conflict?

• Strongly agree • Agree • Disagree • Strongly disagree	• I defend my point of view no matter what • I seek the support of a third person (manager, HR, mentor) • I take responsibility for the conflict and see it as an opportunity for me to evolve my thinking • I put my opinion aside and attempt to understand the other's point of view • I accept that person's opinion without judgment • I move ahead anyway when I believe that is the right thing to do • I ignore conflicts in order to preserve harmony with others

At the end of these 6 months, we had an overall framework broken down into 23 different measures. We had an extensive list of questions that could be clustered in a multitude of ways to inform the scores. We had created the foundation of a product that was sourced from our unique life experiences and designed to make our lofty visions more relevant and accessible to organizations.

These six months were without doubt the most fun and productive of my working career. When I think back on them, they appear as a blur. We had entered into such a flow, similar to what artists must feel when they are creating from a deep place of connection and inspiration. We often talk about this creation process as something being channeled through us. Sujith and I happened to be the right people at the right time to "receive" it and bring it into form, but we never felt we "owned" it. Therefore, right from the beginning, we chose not to copyright any of this material, despite being advised to do so by many people.

These adapted words by Kahlil Gibran ring true when thinking about our creative process:

> *Something comes through you*
> *But it is not from you*
> *And though it is with you*
> *It belongs not to you*

At the end of this first creation phase, immediately another one opened up. One of Sujith's many qualities is his ability to think big. He helped me see that the next step was to leverage technology to develop the artificial intelligence that would automatically translate a user's response to the 83 questions into a detailed, personalized report. This was a bold vision but, given the flow we were in, we decided to take on the challenge.

Sujith's connection to India opened the door to some of the most brilliant tech resources I have ever worked with. For the next six months we were fully immersed in creating the intelligence of the tool and the backend structure that would enable the automation and scaling of this work in the future. At this point we were feeling the huge potential of what lied ahead. We were ready to formalize our business and commit to a partnership. We were ready to go to market.

QUESTIONS FOR THE BEING ENTREPRENEUR:

- What new product or service are you uniquely qualified to bring into the world?

- In what way is it a perfect integration of all of your past experiences?

- What steps can you take today to build a prototype that is sharable with your target audience?

8. Building the bridge

A Being Entrepreneur accepts that it is 100% their responsibility to build the bridge into their client's reality (versus expecting them to meet us halfway). This does not mean diluting our idea, so it's more easily understood. Instead, we must access a next level of ingenuity, a place where we can reconcile our highest aspirations with their most basic needs. It's when this bridge has been built, that tangible results finally start to flow.

It didn't take long for two pilot clients to come on board. One of them was an innovative travel agency based in the Netherlands and the other was a Swiss based NGO. In both cases the data from the HQ survey revealed some very powerful insights.

The story that was emerging out of the analysis for the travel agency was showing a decrease in their willingness to experiment with new ideas. They had become more risk averse and the bold vision of the founders was no longer permeating throughout the rapidly expanding organization. As the diagram below clearly shows, finding a way to re-inspire the organization's entrepreneurial roots, while maintaining the stability of their core business, was the key tension they needed to work with.

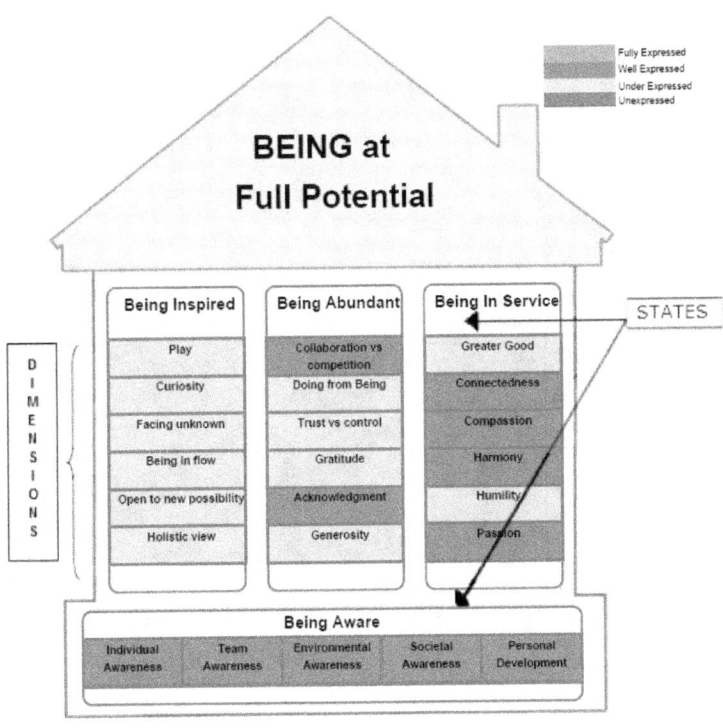

For the Swiss based NGO, the data revealed a slightly more uncomfortable truth. There seemed to be a gap between their Being and Doing. This was a group of highly aware individuals. They all had a wealth of experience and had invested significantly in their personal growth. In the data though we could see that this high individual awareness was both a potential strength AND weakness. On the one hand, people would look up to them as experts / wise men and women. This was of course an important asset for the consultancy work they do with senior business and political leaders. However, on the other hand, we observed lower scores in the area of Personal Development. It seemed that their expert status was keeping them from questioning themselves and embracing a learning mindset. It was a fascinating tension that we confronted them with when we presented their Heart Quotient House profile.

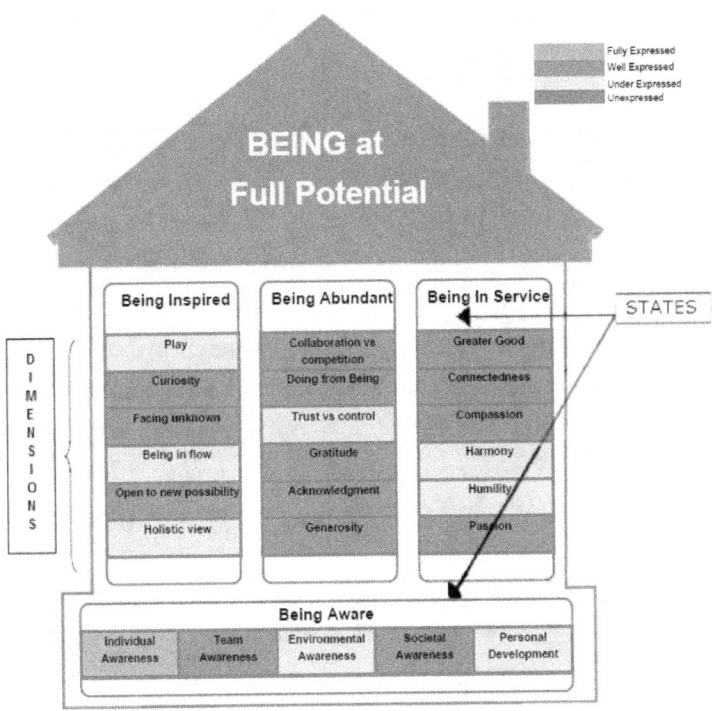

I remember the senior members of the group reacting in quite a skeptical and defensive way to these findings. However, the younger people were absolutely thrilled with these insights. They couldn't believe how clearly the data was speaking to this intuitive knowing they had inside. In their heart they knew something wasn't right but until now they had not been able to articulate it.

Both of these clients had experienced a similar kind of effect - the data was validating what their gut knew was true. We started to realize that the value of our proposition was to bring to the surface, and objectively measure, the more subtle organizational dynamics that we know are important but, until now, rarely get acted on. By making our intuitive knowing visible and measurable we could enable organizations to start having new conversations, new insights and ultimately new behaviors.

As a result of this piloting phase we picked up another important lesson that would change the way we talk about and position this work in the future. Even though the name "Heart Quotient" accurately described what we were doing, it was not the language that had the most traction with the people we were trying to serve. It was definitely easier to comprehend than the "Inner Voice" but still not relevant enough for the mainstream organizations we envisioned working with. Acknowledging and accepting this, once again, opened the way to more creativity. We asked ourselves how we can refer to this deeper work in a way that inspires our target group yet still aligns with the true essence of our approach?

Albert Einstein once said: "If I had an hour to solve a problem, and my life depended on the solution, I would spend the first 55 mins determining the proper question to ask...for once I know the proper question, I could solve the problem in less than 5 mins".

This was absolutely true in our case. The alternative to the Heart Quotient name came instantly once we opened up to it. From then on, we would be referring to the assessment, and all the work related to it, as Human Potential Realization. The Heart Quotient score was now the Human Potential score. The official company name: Human Potential Development INC. and the brand we would position ourselves under: BEING at Full Potential.

Shortly after the pilot experiences I arranged to meet up with my friend and mentor from the corporate world. I was excited to share with her the big breakthroughs since our last chat when the HQ idea came up. She was amazed with all the progress and very intrigued with the two case studies we had just completed. She could see the possibilities to bring it into teams but first wanted to experience and better understand the work herself. So together with her HR Director, she signed up for the Human Potential certification training we had recently developed. This was a 4-week online course to enable like-minded coaches and Organizational development experts to become proficient in bringing the assessment and Human Potential methodology to their clients or within their organizations. We knew that for this work to expand in the world we had to create an open system where our partners could easily access the tools and resources, they needed to integrate Human Potential realization into their value proposition.

At the end of the course I remember having an extensive feedback session with my previous colleagues. They loved what we had developed but there was a missing piece that would have to be addressed before organizations like theirs could commit. She challenged us to find a way to connect the depth of the model with the things that keep leaders up at night. In other words, could we expand the House framework in a way that intuitively shows the interconnectedness of our deep human aspirations and the strategic priorities of organizations. Given our extensive experience in the corporate world we were well aware what those strategic priorities were. Every leader will agree that innovation, customer satisfaction, employee engagement and trustworthiness are critical drivers of the business. They easily acknowledge that excelling in these areas will automatically lead to breakthroughs in performance.

This triggered another wave of creativity resulting in what we now refer to as the ICEBERG model. With this framework we were able to distinguish between the visible and invisible drivers of a business. This made it much simpler to understand how the deeper human potential development work connects and enables the key business drivers that organizational leaders relate to.

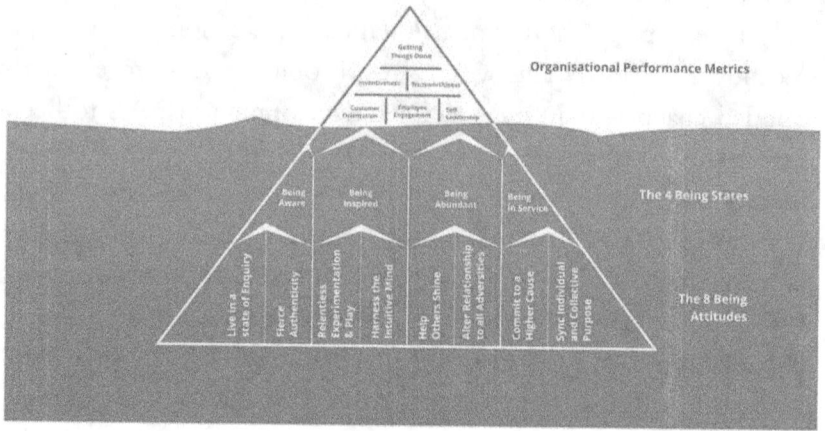

In addition to telling a much more integrated story we also found a way to reconfigure the 83 questions so that the additional "above the water" organizational performance metrics could also be quantified. Was this the holy grail of organizational transformation?

My previous boss seemed to think so. During my next visit with her, approximately 6 years after I had resigned, everything clicked. Within minutes of showing her the iceberg and how we had broken down each of the organizational performance metrics into concrete phases of development that organizations could assess themselves on, she said "Yes".

Example: breakdown of OPM "Inventiveness"

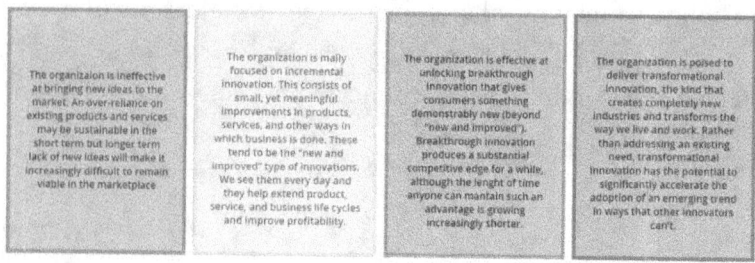

The bridge connecting our vision to her needs had now been built. Shortly thereafter, we signed a project with her newly formed Global Sustainability Team which consisted of a Human Potential assessment, individual debrief sessions with each team member and a 3-day workshop at their headquarters in Cincinnati.

For me personally, this was a profound moment of arrival. The lofty dream I had set for myself when I left the organization in 2010 had now become a reality. The circle was complete. Here's an extract of the learnings we captured after the 3-day workshop. These lessons would continue to inform our work with future clients.

LESSON #1: Location is nothing, our BEING is everything

We can easily assume that this kind of deep work should happen well outside the confines of the day to day business environment. We therefore invest significantly in finding the "perfect" off-site location that we feel supports the deepening into our personal and collective growth. No doubt that a beautiful location can help to disconnect and inspire us to open up.

The problem with this approach is that our heightened state of BEING is associated with the environment in which it was created.

Therefore, when participants head back to the office after the workshop they quickly revert back to old patterns and behaviors.

We have found that, when done correctly, it can be even more powerful to hold the workshop in the heart of the day to day business operations. Not only is this the best way to prepare people for post-workshop immersion, but it also creates a powerful "energetic" spill over into the rest of the office. People literally feel the ripples and are positively impacted by the vibes coming from the workshop space.

In order for this to work it helps to set clear guidelines on what is expected from the participants. We have found that two simple commitments create a solid foundation for introducing this work in any office environment:

- Privacy and confidentiality: even though the workshop room can be in the midst of the day-to-day business environment we must ensure that there is sufficient privacy to create the necessary safety for participants
- All participants commit to full engagement for the duration of the workshop. Staying in the office can increase the temptation to drop in and out of the program while keeping an eye on the business.

LESSON #2: Infuse mysticism but don't keep it mysterious

It can be scary to bring in new practices and rituals like sitting in a circle with a candle at the center and adopting the use of a listening stick. Especially in the business context we easily assume this is taboo and that it will be rejected by workshop participants.

Our experience is proving the contrary. However, there is one big caveat. If we assume people will simply accept it and unhesitatingly go along with it then it probably will not work. However, if we openly acknowledge that we are doing things differently and clearly explain

WHY we are doing it that way then the taboo is instantly removed. In doing so we can easily move these new practices from the esoteric realm to a deeper level of humanism.

For example, to help understand the reason for sitting together in a circle with a candle at the center we can tell the story of the Children's Fire - a decision making process predating the Mayans of Central America. These people established a deep democratic system of governance known as the Circle of Law and implemented a circular wisdom decision making structure, known as the Council, to facilitate this.

In the very center of this structure they placed a small fire which was to remind the eight pairs of representatives (or Chiefs as they were known) that the primary consideration should always be the continuation of life when making decisions of any kind. They called this seemingly insignificant fire, The Children's Fire and lived by the simple principle: LIFE FIRST. To bring greater focus to our future generations, council members would hold the question, "what kind of world do we want our children, and our children's children, to inherit?" before making any significant decisions. This system even inspired the original constitution of the USA.

Intentionally embodying this same spirit of service to future generations can be a powerful ritual to bring back into the organizational work of today.

LESSON #3: Invest in BEING, unleash the DOING

"I know of no more encouraging fact than the unquestionable ability of man to elevate his life by a conscious endeavor. It is something to be able to paint a particular picture, or to carve a statue, and so to make a few objects beautiful; but it is far more glorious to carve and paint the very atmosphere and medium through

which we look. To affect the quality of the day, that is the highest of arts". Henry David Thoreau

Taking quality time to "step into BEING" is an absolute prerequisite to any transformational workshop. This process of slowing down sharpens our individual and collective presence. As we practice mindfulness techniques, set collective standards of engagement, and get to know each other at a deeper level, it may feel like we are distracting ourselves from key business and organizational priorities. However, in reality this investment in BEING is creating the conditions for participants to access deeper levels of knowing (intuition) and transcend some limiting beliefs and assumptions they may have about the way things ARE or SHOULD BE.

Through this process we are preparing ourselves to look at the business and organizational challenges through a new lens. As Albert Einstein once famously said:

"We cannot solve our problems with the same thinking we used when we created them". A. Einstein

By the end of day 1 (of a 2- or 3-day workshop), when our BEING is fully ignited and awareness heightened, we will experience an intense creative tension in the group. There will be an unstoppable urge to move our BEINGNESS into DOINGNESS. Like a spring that has been wound up and is ready to be released, we will be inspired to unleash our full creative potential on any task assigned to us. (for example creating a long term vision or purpose for the team, defining strategies and action planning, or crafting the new language and rituals that will shape the culture of the organization going forward.

When this DOINGNESS is coming from a place of deep BEINGNESS then it will feel effortless and efficient, while triggering a high level of commitment and alignment amongst workshop participants.

LESSON #4: Use Human Potential DATA to break open conversations and unlock new thinking

Prior to these discovery workshops each participant is invited to take the Human Potential Assessment. This gives us concrete data points on how well expressed the individual and collective potential is. Coming into the workshop there is typically a high level of curiosity and eagerness to dive into the findings. However, we have learnt that timing is everything when it comes to introducing the data into the conversation. It can have a significant impact on how it is interpreted and utilized.

"Most executives, many scientists, and almost all business school graduates believe that if you analyze data, this will give you new ideas. Unfortunately, this belief is totally wrong. The mind can only see what it is prepared to see". Edward de Bono

For example, if we engage with the assessment results right from the beginning, without first elevating our state of BEING, then we will likely look at the data with an analytical mind and apply assumptions that simply reinforce our current reality. However, if we hold off sharing the data until the workshop participants have fully immersed in a heightened state of awareness, then they will also engage with the data and findings in more transformational ways. Rather than simply using their analytical mind, they now also approach the interpretation of findings in a more expanded, intuitive way. We have demonstrated over and over again that the insights ensuing from this approach have the potential to unleash, and sustain, a new wave of inspiration in the organization.

LESSON #5: No matter how profound the collective experience is it needs to be accompanied with on-going work at the individual level in order to sustain itself

This expansion of BEING that happens in most of our workshops and trainings typically opens the door to a collective expansion as well. Participants feel united in their journey and inspired to join forces around a collective cause. These are always extremely powerful moments of deep connection with each other and alignment to a greater purpose. It gives meaning to our lives, and in that moment, it is easy to step beyond our fears and trust the natural unfolding of the collective energy.

Although we have glimpsed the collective Gold and genuinely embraced the intention to make it happen, sooner or later our individual journey starts coming in the way. Our fears, that seemed irrational just a few days ago, are once again holding us back and drawing us into old patterns. Now the collective potential is put on hold while we take the next step on our individual journeys. So, we must learn to reconnect time and again: with ourselves, with others and with the collective. That requires enhancing our awareness and actually choosing to practice reconnecting. This will benefit our individual response ability to meet life in all its aspects and contribute to our individual and collective journey.

This incredible experience was a sign that we were now ready to confidently step into the organizational development (OD) playing field and position ourselves as credible Human Potential experts / transformation agents. Within the next couple of years our network of certified coaches grew exponentially and without much traditional marketing & sales effort, clients of all sizes and sectors signed up to work with us.

It was fascinating to observe how this deep human work had universal appeal. We attracted clients from Mexico, US, India, New Zealand and all across Europe. The depth of our approach seemed to effortlessly cut through the surface level differences (like race, gender, culture, religion etc...) and naturally connect us at a deeper human level (we all aspire for meaning, fulfillment and the full expression of who we are). Here are some examples of work we did between 2017 and 2019:

Human Potential coach training in Mexico to prepare a group of coaches and consultants for the deployment of the Human Potential Assessment within the National Banking Commission of Mexico (CNBV)

Various Human Potential certification trainings in India

Client workshops in the Netherlands, Italy, Switzerland and the UK.

THE BEING ENTREPRENEUR

Coach trainings in Netherlands and Switzerland

Human Potential Summits for innovation and sustainability

Yearly strategy meetings

The final confirmation that our work was now resonating with visionary leaders was when we received a spontaneous email from Laura Saldivar Luna in San Antonio Texas. As she was getting ready for her new role as Chief People Officer for a US based nonprofit organization, she came across the Being at Full Potential website and decided to reach out with the following message. Since then the relationship with this organization has flourished and they have now become one of our favorite clients.

THE BEING ENTREPRENEUR

My name is Laura Saldivar Luna. I work for an American education organization called Teach For America, which is a partner organization in the global network Teach For All.

In January of 2019, I will formally take on the role of Chief People Officer for my organization, responsible for all human capital work, organizational culture work, diversity and inclusion work, and the traditional human resources functions typically found in most organizations. We have ~1,800 employees who are responsible for delivering programmatic impact to 60,000+ members of our leadership network.

I'm using the next few months of 2018 to prepare myself for this new role. In my reading and writing this evening, I stumbled upon your website as I was searching for methodologies for measuring human potential. I'm very interested in learning more about your frameworks, methodology, and services. I'd also like to know if the training opportunity offered in the Netherlands next month is the type of experience well-suited for a novice to the model.

A little about me—I've worked for my organization for 13+ years and started as an entry-level employee. I currently work as an Executive Director of one of our regional sites, located in the city where I grew up (San Antonio, Texas, USA). I'm a wife and mother to two toddlers (ages 2 and 3), am a certified Yoga instructor (not currently teaching though) and am a member of the Aspen Institute's Global Leadership Network. I've just come off of a couple of weeks of intensive training in a methodology for executive reinvention that focuses on an ontological approach to pursuing transformation. I'm currently obsessed with how we, as leaders, must be grounded in who we are BEING as opposed to our normal approach of focusing on the DOING. I want to make this a cornerstone of the strategy I pursue in my new role leading our People Team.

What I read on your website resonates with me, and I'm wondering if you have any materials, you'd be willing to share with me so I can learn more. While I have no doubt that you have no shortage of current and potential clients, the work I will soon take on as Chief People Officer of Teach For America will be a full commitment to BEING a transformational leader who develops other transformational leaders. I think we might have a lot in common!

Let me know how I can learn more about your work.

Laura

QUESTIONS FOR THE BEING ENTREPRENEUR:

- How would you describe the barriers you face as an entrepreneur when it comes to getting the attention of your target audience?

- In what ways can these barriers be a springboard for new creativity and innovation?

- How will you know when that bridge to your ideal client has been built?

9. Back to source

To a Being Entrepreneur, manifesting a vision is not only a celebratory moment of arrival, but it's also an invitation to embrace the next adventure. Once again, we are compelled to let go of the known, open up to new possibilities, stretch the limits of our imagination, and take the next step on our journey to self realization.

Around 2019, almost 10 years after embarking on this journey, I could feel that the next cycle of growth was just around the corner. If it took 10 years of market research experience with a large multinational to prepare myself for Being at Full Potential, then perhaps it would also take these last 10 years of entrepreneurship to prepare for the next step on my life's journey.

In my heart I knew something new was coming through but intellectually it didn't make sense yet. Didn't I just arrive? With all these exciting opportunities, shouldn't I just be content and enjoy the ride? It didn't make sense, so I continued with business as usual. However, before long, the heart came back, this time knocking at the door a little bit louder. It wanted to be heard, it had an important message for me.

This back and forth between the heart and the mind went on for several months until one day I surrendered and opened up to the messages coming through. Something about the status quo was no longer aligned with my deeper aspirations. I had lost connection with the fun and joy that had fueled this incredible adventure. Relationships were no longer flowing, and conversations were strained.

For example, one of the conversations we'd been having with the core team was the idea of scaling up and creating more impact. We referred to it as "going exponential" or the "quantum leap". We spoke about reaching millions of people in the coming years. However, these aspirational words did not lead to any action. We couldn't fully sense it in our guts. Therefore, we remained stuck, going around in circles and feeling frustrated. Dialing down the goal to a more realistic target was not the solution to reignite the energy. Something more fundamental needed to be addressed before we could start dreaming about the next frontiers.

This is when the Covid pandemic appeared. From one day to the next everything slowed down. The sense of urgency to reach new heights was put on hold, creating space to reengage in the deeper conversations and reconnect with our individual yearnings. It was in these quieter moments that the real insights could come through. We courageously acknowledged that something was dying, and that we had to hold space for this process before something new could start coming through.

This is when, one day, Sujith, my friend and partner in this work for the past 10 years, announced that he was stepping out. Despite all the good reasons to stay involved, he was able to honor the deeper knowing inside that it was time to refocus his energy on other projects that were closer to his heart. His departure left a void.

It's only when I stepped into the emptiness of the void that I could sense the exponential leaps and quantum shifts, that we had been talking about just a few weeks back, had now been set in motion.

I felt lonely, but free. Everything was back on the table to be looked at with fresh eyes. Assumptions and beliefs that had driven our way of working until now could be reexamined and realigned based on the new energy and ideas that were now starting to flow again. Dwelling in the void was also an opportunity to renew relationships and rediscover each other's passion.

So here I am, once again spending time in between the old and the new, just like I did 10 years ago. Even though sometimes it feels like nothing concrete is happening, I know that, at an energetic level, mountains are being moved and that a new foundation is being laid for the future potential to unfold. A new adventure has begun, a new story is waiting to be told.

This is the story of the Being Entrepreneur.

QUESTIONS FOR THE BEING ENTREPRENEUR:

- Where on your entrepreneurial journey to you see opportunity to create more space and innocently be in a place of not knowing?

- What do you need to let go of or say goodbye to?

- Can you sense an invitation for your next adventure as a Being Entrepreneur?

THE BEING ENTREPRENEUR

ABOUT THE AUTHOR

Mark Vandeneijnde is the co-founder of a global assessment and coaching organization, called BEING at Full Potential. In this role he helps leaders (in business, non-profits and government) access and unlock the full HUMAN potential of their organizations. Much of this work requires translating the new, emerging organizational paradigms into concrete, relevant and easy to understand solutions for the realities of today's executives.

As an innovator, bridging these two worlds, Mark has learnt some very valuable lessons about what it takes to succeed as a BEING entrepreneur.

www.ingramcontent.com/pod-product-compliance
Lightning Source LLC
Chambersburg PA
CBHW070240220526
45465CB00004B/1462